SOUL
OF A SWIMMER

By Carla Albano

Soul of a Swimmer

Cover Design & Interior Layout: Nicole Wurtele

Cover photo: Dave Brewington, Aboobarley photography, Coral Springs Florida

All photos courtesy of Carla Albano unless otherwise noted

Published by CG Sports Publishing

A Division of The CG Sports Company
Cejih Yung, CEO and Founder
www.cgsportsco.com

ISBN: 978-1-7359193-6-2

Quantity order requests can be emailed to:
Publishing@cgsportsmanagement.com

Printed in The United States of America

Author's Note

This is a true story about Nicholas Dworet, a swimmer whose life unexpectedly and tragically ended at age 17. Apart from the prologue, the book is a fact-based story derived from interviews with Nick's family, coaches, and friends.

When necessary, content was added to clarify and bridge the facts, intended to be consistent with the spirit of Nick's story. In some cases, the timing and precise language could not be replicated, but all efforts were used to maintain editorial integrity.

For Mommy, Daddy, and Alex

PROLOGUE

~~~~~~~~~

Dec. 14, 2018

Dear Nick,

I miss you today and every day. I glance into your quiet and empty room and smile at the medals still hanging by your bed. The Post-it notes written to yourself are neatly placed alongside photos of Daria, just where you left them. I also love to look at the fortunes from the Chinese cookies you taped to your closet door. They've since yellowed. We should've had the opportunity to see some of those fortunes come true, but we've been deprived of this.

You'd be in college now. When I hear my phone ding, I wonder if it is a text from you about Christmas, but then I remind myself that that's not possible. I smile when I think about discussing your happiest secret, the worst-kept secret it turns out, of Daria thinking about grad school in Indiana. I know you were going to share that news with us at Christmas. Sadly, we never got to have this conversation.

I profoundly miss watching you swim. Your body always rotated through the water with grace. In a warm-up pool of hundreds of swimmers, I could spot your distinctively strong strokes. I miss your excitement about competing. Just before your race, you often asked me to hold your Lokai bracelet. Others and I noticed this was the only time you ever removed your bracelet. After your heat, you would return to me and hug me tightly, always breathlessly. Your heart was beating so hard that it felt like it was going to escape from your chest. It never mattered that you were soaking wet and I was dry, or if it was cold out. It mattered only that we shared these moments together. The harder your heart beat, the closer I wanted to hold you. You were always happy after racing, regardless of the outcome. Memories of your swimming is all I have. I will never SEE you swim again.

If Daddy, Alex, and I were lucky enough to have you home for Christmas, we would swim in your other favorite pool, the ocean at Deerfield Beach. I promise, we would stay as long as you want, all day and night, if needed. I know how much you loved the warm Florida ocean. You'd probably ready for a break from the Indiana cold. It's not possible to revisit all our holiday traditions together. It's just too hard for everyone to carry on.

Daddy thinks about you constantly. He wonders what it would have been like to hear about your new friends, classmates, and teammates. He smiles proudly when he thinks about how successful you would have been at day trading. We'd planned to give you money for Christmas so you had more to invest, but that, too, will never come to be.

There are so many more thoughts I need to share with you and conversations we never got to have. A mother is never ready to say goodbye to her child. So, by writing to you, I continue at least to have a one-sided conversation. Hej då, my boy.

I love you,

Mamma

Note: It's impossible for me to send this and the countless letters I have written before it and the countless letters I will write in the future.

Bullets pierced the chest of our beloved Nick on Feb. 14, 2018, while he was in his last class of the day at Marjory Stoneman Douglas High School in Parkland, Fla.

Nick had little warning. He did not suffer. He died quickly. Nick was a random casualty of a former student who took away Nick's dreams and the dreams of 16 other people that day. He almost killed my other son, Alex, too. With Nick and the others gone, our society is missing countless good things. My son's memory and legacy cannot be erased, though. This is the extraordinary story of Nicholas Paul Dworet.

CHAPTER ONE:
THE MODERN VILLAGE

"Most say it takes a village to raise a champion. But you first need a group of like-minded parents raising the future, whatever the future may hold."

– Anonymous

It was closing time at the pool one sultry afternoon, when the moms were gathering up toys, shoes, bottles, and cranky toddlers long overdue for their naps. It was August 2003, way before the concept of a designated "water watcher" had evolved. A water watcher is a dedicated adult in addition to the lifeguards who observes a playgroup or family of children. Annika thought Nicole, her new friend, was watching their four-and-a-half-year-old boys, and Nicole thought Annika was. Almost in unison, the two moms realized neither was watching, and they turned in terror to see Nicholas and Leif, hand in hand at the edge of the deep end of the pool. It was too far for the moms to run, too noisy for them to scream, and as time stood still, Annika passed her infant son, Alex, to Nicole and tore toward the boys. The boys jumped. They sank. The lifeguard jumped in to retrieve them.

As the lifeguard pushed them to the surface, Nick and Leif emerged from the water thrusting their arms up in the air, triumphant. They were giggling while the lifeguard assisted them toward the ladder. The boys intended to do an encore. Annika who had slowed to a walk by now, was joined by Nicole. Nicole's and Annika's hearts were pounding, and they appeared out of breath. Soon their fear turned to relief, which turned to joy, which turned to cheers. Hurriedly, Nick and Leif ran to jump again, only to be stopped by another lifeguard's whistle. Swimming was over for the day. As the moms' heart rates began to decline and their breathing slowed, they faced each other with nervous smiles and realized the special bond they had instantly formed. The young moms had just survived a near tragedy.

Annika Dworet had only met Nicole Nilsson a few weeks earlier at Mullins Park. New to Coral Springs, Fla., Annika loved to walk to the park from her new home a short distance away, sauntering hand in hand with Nicholas, while she pushed young Alex in the stroller. Eager to make new friends, Annika would enter the busy playground and space herself equidistantly from the other moms, many also new to the neighborhood. Looking over their brows while catching pacifiers, each mom discreetly sized up the others. Simple things such as so-and-so appears to be a nanny or an au-pair versus so-and-so who appears to be a mommy. The mothers observed who was smoking a cigarette, what language people spoke, and any unusual clothing — all of this created a hierarchy and positioning around the playground. Then there were the subtle judgments made about the other parents' attention to child safety. Certainly, inattention to one's child eliminated the parent from being worthy of a conversation. Being an inattentive parent stirred up whispers among strangers, and permanent shunning from any possible new friendships.

One day, Nicole, a loquacious brunette with beautiful curls, approached Annika and asked, "Why do you have your son in Swedish moccasins in this 95-degree heat?" Referring to 9-month-old Alex Dworet, Nicole was right. It was a terribly hot day and Alex was likely stifling. Having his feet covered only added to his discomfort.

Annika and Nicole had seen each other before and had politely observed their sons playing from afar. Shocked by Nicole's knowledge of infant footwear, Annika broke out in a wide smile and asked, "How do YOU know what Swedish moccasins are?" All the while, Annika had sensed Nicole wasn't Swedish, but she soon discovered that Nicole was married to Swede Bo Nilsson, thus her familiarity with Swedish moccasins. Obviously, each woman had passed each other on the shunning test, and Annika and Nicole became fast friends. They closed the space between them on the park bench and started a conversation which has continued now for two decades.

That first summer, the two new friends began to spend most of their time at the pool where their oldest boys thrived. In particular, Nick yearned for the water from the moment he woke until the moment he was ready for bed. Leif, Nicole's oldest son, was Nick's first friend. Leif became the leader of the two, but was the less comfortable swimmer. However, Leif soon embraced the structured Swim America program as much as Nick did. As the summer wore on, the mothers wore out because it became increasingly difficult to get the boys out of the pool. So they gave in and began to pack their lunches, staying for most of the day. Nick soon outgrew the lessons designed for 4-year-olds and moved up to groups designed for much older children. The staff at the pool noticed Nick's talent and suggested to Annika that she pursue the advanced Swim America steps for her son. New to town, Annika was just happy that Nick was happy, and she was content to have an awesome new friend with whom she had a lot in common.

By the end of the summer, Nick had counted the number of tiles around the pool and knew exactly how many were cracked. He knew each lifeguard by name. The smiles on their faces when they saw Nick approaching were endearing, as if their little brother had arrived after a long absence. Nick hung around the lifeguard stands, swinging from the footrests high above his head. He begged the lifeguards to let him sit in their chairs, and occasionally on a slow day, a lifeguard would hoist him up and secure Nick on his lap. Although this was against the rules, young Nick was a special boy, deserving of this treat. Sometimes he wanted to jump from the chair into the pool. Thankfully, that never happened. It was a sweet but way-too-short summer.

The Dworet family's journey to the summer of 2003 began about a decade earlier. In 1989, Annika Persson, the middle daughter of Nils and Birgitta Persson, left her parents' home in Sweden for the first time to travel to Los Angeles to become an au pair.

She left behind her innocent beginnings in Nora, a village of just over 12,000 people in northern Sweden. Her hometown was founded in 1643. It is known for its wooden homes and cobblestone streets. For centuries, the village flourished; modernity had bypassed it. Local lore was that the village was special because in almost 400 years it had not succumbed to fire, which certainly would have devoured the cherished historic homes. In 1856, Nora became one of the initial stops on the first coal-burning railway in Sweden, an artifact of local pride.

Nora mostly subsisted on the mining industry, which was established there in the 1700s. Later, apple farming became a secondary industry. Nearby is Lake Norasjön, the main body of fresh water. It includes an island with a recreational area. In spring and summer, Annika thrived in the verdant countryside, passing through beautiful orchards on her way to the lake. The lake was clear and clean, fueled by cold streams, the result of runoff from the mountains. As the summer progressed, the runoff slowed and the lake warmed. Friendships grew among the local children. Memories of these friendships sustained many a Swede through the long and difficult winters with visions of when they could return and pick up where they had left off, enjoying the lake year after year.

Annika was a beautiful blonde girl with long legs and a shy smile that revealed blue eyes that competed with the color of the lake. She was a natural swimmer, favoring the breaststroke. She swam daily in the summer. She tanned easily, and by summer's end seemed ready for the paleness coming with winter ahead.

Leaving the comfort of Nora, Annika was excited about the stories other au pairs had shared. She mostly wanted to live in the present and experience the famous California weather which she believed would enable her to maintain year-round tan. Annika also wanted to take time off after secondary school, which was strict and difficult in Sweden. She was excited about seeing another part of the world and fulfilling a contract working for an American family. Annika then expected to return to Sweden to study nursing. She never envisioned immigrating to the United States.

Annika didn't understand what an eye-opening experience she would encounter by becoming an au pair in Los Angeles. The allure of the large city, an endless populous of interesting young people, and the enticing

California lifestyle quickly enchanted her. She discovered the Pacific Ocean, which was a mesmerizing force. "Is this what love feels like?" she thought. She first lived with a family near Huntington Beach and could sometimes smell the salt air while dreaming of the sea when she wasn't able to feel the sand between her toes. Her host family enjoyed the ocean and, when able, they would all travel to the beach for an afternoon respite. It was there on the shore where Annika would chase after toddlers with the sun capturing her beautiful blonde highlights. As summer turned to fall, there never seemed to be a change in season. Then it was time for Annika to return home to Sweden for Christmas.

Upon landing in snowbound Stockholm that first Christmas, Annika was met by her family and a two-hour car journey west to their home in Nora. As she looked outside over the snow drifts imagining blue skies and Pacific waves, Annika realized she had outgrown Sweden, and that large-city living, such as in Los Angeles and its suburbs, would provide her the excitement, lifestyle, and opportunities she desired. By the end of her short trip home, and as much as she tried to envision life again in Nora, Annika sadly realized that she could never return to live in her small Swedish village.

Following her contract as an au pair, Annika entered nursing school at Santa Monica City College. She shared an apartment with several other students, each working part time. When seeking flexible employment at a local restaurant, Annika met the manager, Mitch Dworet, who questioned her experience waiting tables. Prodded by his fellow staff, Mitch took a chance and hired her. They worked together and played together. Play led to love.

Mitch, nearly a decade Annika's senior, was a physical specimen from Southern California. Fit and handsome, he was a devoted workout buff who also loved the culinary arts. He respected his body both inside and out through a regimented fitness program, careful diet, and introspection — now known as mindfulness. As a teenager, Mitch migrated to California from New York with his small, close-knit family. Mitch had been raised in a conservative Jewish family, but as an adult formulated an individual and personal spiritual base. He hadn't drifted from Judaism, but rather privatized his beliefs and made them sacred. He worshiped frequently and had a healthy mind reinforced by meditation.

Mitch was fortunate to have been educated at one of the finest culinary institutes in Santa Barbara, California. Second to Annika, the restaurant business was Mitch's passion. Mitch had all of the qualities it took to run a successful restaurant. He had worked in some of the most notable dining establishments in Los Angeles, including the legendary Chasen's, a restaurant frequented by Hollywood stars. Mitch had an eclectic mix of friends, many of whom were connected and engaged in the entertainment business. One would never know it because he was humble and reserved. Mitch was personable and smart. He listened before he spoke. He had piercing brown eyes. When he made eye contact, he engaged and connected with others on an intimate level. There was nothing superficial about Mitch; he was genuine and intense. Annika and Mitch were a good match; they completed one another.

By the time Mitch and Annika met, Mitch was a much-accomplished runner and bicyclist in Southern California. He aspired to do triathlons. Swimming was the weakest leg of Mitch's triathlon, and running was by far his strongest. Mitch loved to work out along the Los Angeles coastline. It was normal for him to bike from Malibu to Palos Verdes — a nearly 40-mile one-way trek — and back when he had free time. He also enjoyed running on the numerous hillside trails in the Santa Monica Mountains and in Santa Barbara. Mitch would often compete in running races of any distance from five kilometers up to marathons. He was a visible and respected area athlete. Later in life, he became a certified personal trainer so that he could share health and wellness with others. Mitch was friendly and outgoing, and mentored other runners and bicyclists. Mitch was always in search of tips to improve his swimming, a word that made him smile but also quiver.

After Annika graduated from nursing school, they married at a small neighborhood chapel. They lived happily in a rent-controlled, one-bedroom apartment in Santa Monica. Santa Monica was positioned perfectly for the couple to pursue their passions — biking, running, and sometimes swimming. They regularly exercised together and found great pleasure in exploring the neighborhoods, foothills, and the Santa Monica Mountains on foot or on bike. When it came to swimming, they often chose the pool. Mitch also taught Annika how to rollerblade, which became a perfect hobby they shared together on the Santa Monica boardwalk.

Two Became Three

After being married for a short time and settled into their careers and active lives, Mitch and Annika were thrilled to learn they would be adding a baby to their family. This would be the first grandchild on Mitch's side of the family. Mitch's parents were extremely excited and helpful in preparing their son to become a father, drawing upon their faith for much of their advice and knowledge.

For centuries, teachings of the Torah sought to explain the wonders of human development. In 1948, with a modern twist, screenwriter Richard Brooks was given the task to rescript lines for Humphrey Bogart for the movie "Key Largo." A fleeting part of the script described a baby in the womb being infused with all the knowledge and wisdom he or she needs in life. An angel then comes to quiet the child and places her finger upon his upper lip, creating an indentation that symbolizes the completion of the acquisition of knowledge and wisdom, thus the reason for the philtrum. Greeks call it a "love charm."

Fondly remembering this teaching from his childhood, Mitch knew his baby would be special, filled with extraordinary knowledge and wisdom. He found comfort and serenity in watching Annika grow with their baby. It was a magical time.

Annika and Mitch chose to learn the gender of their first born upon its arrival. As the time came closer to meet their baby, Annika's mom,

Birgitta, traveled for the first time by herself from Sweden. Usually only one family member was allowed in the delivery room, but the hospital made an exception so that both Mitch and Birgitta could be present.

When Annika went into labor, Mitch and Birgitta set up a video camera to record the birth. Annika later needed a cesarean delivery, and Mitch quickly relocated the camera. When Nicholas made his entrance, Mitch and Birgitta were so excited that as they were celebrating, they inadvertently blocked the view of the camera that was rolling behind them. The video recorded the backs of Mitch and Birgitta rejoicing in Nicholas' arrival — that was the extent of the videographic memories of Nicholas' birth. Birgitta was the first to hold Nick before passing him to his father and mother. He was a beautiful blond-haired baby, with a perfectly defined "love charm" and a couple of cute dimples. Nick was the dream that came true.

The difficulty of housing in Los Angeles is legendary, so when Nicholas arrived in 2000, Mitch and Annika vacated the only bedroom in their apartment, creating a nursery for Nick. They erected a partition in the living room to create a small living space and a new master bedroom. Their newly renovated apartment proved to be an amazingly happy home.

When a position became available in Mitch's company in Fort Lauderdale, Fla., the Dworets decided to relocate. Carefully analyzing the area for the best schools and location to raise their family, Mitch and Annika decided upon Coral Springs, a suburb just north of Fort Lauderdale, and adjacent to the new suburb of Parkland. Their second son, Alexander, was born in Florida in 2003.

Mitch and Annika were always family-centric, values-driven people. There is the "family they were born with" and "the family that they chose." Choosing new friends in Florida took some time. There were moments of loneliness and longing for the California Mitch and Annika had left behind. But life had changed. They had small children, new jobs and a responsibility to establish their family in a safe and nurturing community.

The recreational and social value of parks is immeasurable; they are the common denominator for people to connect and share with their community. Hence, the profound purpose of Mullins Park, the unofficial welcoming center for newcomers to Coral Springs. Mullins Park provided a sense of community and serenity for the Dworets and for many other families. It was a place to establish roots.

Mullins Park is the largest park in Coral Springs. Named after the developer of Coral Springs, it hosts a variety of sports programs, including soccer, tennis, and swimming. It also has walking trails, a large playground, and space for virtually any outdoor endeavor. The park provides a place where families can experience growth and celebrate athletic milestones.

When Annika met Nicole, she came to understand how important Mullins Park was to the neighborhood and to her budding friendships. Annika and Nicole shared the same desire that their sons explore the outdoors and sports together, and there was no better place to do so than Mullins Park. Secretly, Nicole wished that her son Leif would take to swimming like Nick did.

Annika knew that Nicole would guide her into the Coral Springs community. Nicole was a petite, cute, outgoing stay-at-home mom, always willing to help with a local cause or event. She had many friends and included the Dworets among them. Annika was able to find an empathetic ear in Nicole when she mentioned missing Sweden from time to time, especially around the holidays. The families made it a point to establish holiday traditions based upon their shared Swedish heritage.

As the Nilsson and Dworet boys grew up together at Mullins Park, so did their friendships. The moms enjoyed watching their sons experience many firsts together. There was the first swim meet at the close of the pool season in 2005. It was quite the amateur event, one lap of freestyle only. The kids all lined up and dove (or rather fell in) from the side of the pool. The parents shouted. Annika and Nicole cheered for all the children, to the point of developing dual sore throats. Every young swimmer got a ribbon.

Nick's performance was remarkable, finishing well ahead of the others. His freestyle stroke was aquatic poetry; it was apparent he was special. Afterward, the lifeguards and pool staff gathered around Annika and spoke with her about seeking out a competitive program for Nick. The best beginners were at Mullins Park. More advanced programs were located at the Coral Springs Aquatic Center, which was a few miles north. She smiled, listened, and nodded. Annika took it all in, packed up her children and her stroller, and walked home. All the way home, Nick held his first swimming ribbon tightly in his hand. The ribbon was red with white writing. It had "Mullins Park 2005" stamped into it. He rubbed every edge of the ribbon and stared at it with admiration. Never once did he ask what place he finished. That didn't matter. He slept with the ribbon that night. As he dreamed, and snored little boy snores, Annika carefully removed it from his tightly closed hand and placed it on his dresser.

Besides seeing their boys win their first swimming ribbons, Annika and Nicole experienced their boys losing their first teeth, needing their first stitches, having their first high fevers, and their first broken bones. As a pediatric emergency department nurse, Annika was always a good resource for health-related firsts. But she always admitted it's different when it's your own child, and being a mom was her sacred and primary job. Nicole's children were Annika's children and vice versa; and both nurtured these children in a beautiful way.

The families shared common goals and values for their children. They explored nearly every sport together, including enrolling their sons in tennis. One day, while watching the boys not be attentive to their tennis teacher, swinging their rackets wildly, Annika met another mom, Kathy Searle. Kathy, a native of Australia, quickly became friends with Annika and Nicole. Kathy had just moved to Coral Springs with her husband, Brad, and children Ethan and Mikaela. Her children were the same age as Nick and Alex. Kathy always smiled and was an energetic, thoughtful working mom who ran the family business. Ethan and Nick became soulful friends. Ethan was a polite child who from an early age excelled at his studies. He was destined to perform well in academics rather than in sports. However, Ethan also enjoyed recreational play and was always up for adventures with his new friends. Soon, the three multicultural families, consisting of at least six children, embarked on a variety of adventures together.

The village of families continued to grow. While out bicycling one day, Annika met a young woman named Christine Hiler. The women discovered that they had a lot in common. Besides cycling, they both enjoyed running and had children about the same age. Christine and her husband, Mark Greenwald, had two girls. The couple met in college where both were gymnasts. Mark also enjoyed running, and he and Mitch became running partners. The Greenwalds' first born, Alexandra, would go on to become a talented gymnast.

The Greenwalds introduced the Dworets to competitive running. When the adults decided to enter their first 5k race together, Annika and Christine placed a blanket on the ground at the finish line and plopped all four children down in the middle. Young Nick and Alexandra were put in charge of their younger siblings. The moms said: "Both daddies will be back in about 20 minutes, us moms a few minutes after them. Don't leave the blanket until we return. Promise?" This practice inspired a very fast race for the adults. For the short period of time that it went on, the children were obedient; they never moved.

Nick and Alexandra were not confined to a blanket for long. In 2007, they entered their first competitive 5k at age 7 in the 10-and-under age division. They were excited for the opportunity because the youth age division for similar races typically starts at 14 and under. Each did well. From then on, time permitting, running races became a ritual for the Dworet and Greenwald families.

Alexandra and Nick became lifelong friends. They bonded over their mutual drive for success. They shared a passion for their respective individual sports, and a passion for the outdoors. They made many memories together, including going ice skating and Nick persuading Alexandra to play with Nerf guns instead of Barbie dolls. One of their favorite movies was "Finding Nemo."

Beauty for the Beasts

At one point, Annika and Nicole decided to explore modeling for their boys. They invested in photographs and enlisted contracts with a local modeling agency. There was interest in all of the boys for local photo shoots but the pursuit took too much time and travel, especially with Annika working 12-hour shifts. Further, the notorious Miami traffic could make driving to a photo shoot just miles south of Coral Springs, nerve-wracking and frustrating. So, the opportunity to model became a backburner hobby, even though the agencies chased the boys to come for auditions for nearly a decade. However, Alex Dworet, Nick's younger brother, found much success with modeling. All of the children were photogenic.

Coral Springs had highly rated schools, drawing many families to settle there. Parents also enriched their children's early education with supplemental books, flash cards, and drills. Annika recalled one of her boys' favorite books taught small children the history and flora and fauna of America's 50 states. Nick became particularly interested in Hawaii and could pronounce the name of its state fish, humuhumunukunukuapuaa, perfectly by age 6. Most people use its common name, triggerfish. Throughout his life, Nick took great pride in knowing that he was probably the only person in the room who could correctly pronounce the official name of this fish. Nick's curiosity with this fish led to a lifelong infatuation with Hawaii.

When Nick read the section of the book about Florida, it taught him about alligators and dragonflies. Even though the book made a big deal over Florida's famous amphibious reptiles, Nick showed a preference for dragonflies over alligators while on family adventures. Florida's freshwater bodies create an abundance of dragonflies of various species, but viewing them is tricky. Sometimes Annika would plan special trips at sunrise or twilight (the best times for dragonflies) wishing and hoping that they had hatched so that Nick could be satisfied. Nick's excitement was palpable the closer they got, just like a dog who hears the food bag rattling from the pantry.

Nick knew all about dragonflies. He could recite most of the scientific information a young child could comprehend about their lifecycle. Nick, now favoring the sport of swimming, had found kinship with dragonflies because they live in water for up to five years before becoming an insect for just a mere few weeks. He wanted to be a dragonfly so he too could live mostly in water. Nick's parents were amused by this.

Traditions: New and Old

As all the families became closer, they began to introduce each other to their special holidays and traditions. Although many Swedish holidays are influenced by the Church of Sweden, there were several holidays and traditions that Annika and Bo were happy to celebrate together, and to introduce to the other families.

Frequently, the Dworets and their friends would make trips to the local IKEA store, a Swedish mainstay that served up national favorites in its restaurant. Nick was always quick to request whatever leftovers remained from his friends' plates. Annika liked to buy Nick a popular and less expensive Swedish version of caviar, called Kalles. The children also would select special Swedish chocolate and cookies to take home. IKEA provided unique products when home goods or a gift were needed and sponsored parties in their store for all of the Swedish holidays. When the Dworets chose to celebrate these holidays at home, IKEA sold decorations and tableware specific to the particular holiday, such as kräftskiva.

Kräftskiva, a traditional summertime crayfish party originating in Sweden, was regularly celebrated by the Coral Springs tribe. The party-goers would wear paper party hats and bibs in preparation for a messy meal. The tables were draped with colorful tablecloths and lanterns adorned with Man in the Moon depictions. Eager children circled the kitchen while the crayfish boiled, imagining the crustaceans in their mouths once again.

The crayfish turned a color of lobster red after being boiled alive in salt water and seasoned with fresh dill. They were then dumped in a big pile on a table to be cracked and picked by hand. The dinner table resembled a feeding frenzy with shells and meat flying. There was also bread, mushroom pies, strong Västerbotten cheese, salads, and other dishes.

The Swedish holiday of Midsommar became another village favorite because it coincided with the summer solstice in June. In Sweden, Midsommar is just like a Maypole party, which was a centuries-old tradition originated by Europeans, and later adapted into Swedish culture. Midsommar is a lunch party celebrating the abundance of flowers and the beauty of spring. Women wear flowers in their hair. One of the favorite beverages is flavored schnapps, which can lead to dancing around a pole while the crowd sings. The foods favored at Midsommar include pickled herring served with delightful new potatoes, chives, and sour cream.

The Coral Springs' version of Midsommar involved a family-centered barbecue and celebration, lots of flowers, and beer and wine. However, Nick discovered herring and came to love the smelly fish. The fermented version of herring associated with this holiday is called surströmming. Some say a newly opened can of surströmming has one of the most putrid food smells in the world, even stronger than similarly fermented fish dishes from Asia. Nick became curious but never ate surströmming; he stuck to plain pickled herring.

Meanwhile, it was Nicole Nilsson's job to educate her friends and family on two American holidays: the Fourth of July and Thanksgiving. The Fourth of July melded together with the Midsommar holiday, so Nicole gave up on this holiday. The historical significance of the occasion was lost in what seemed like an every-weekend party, given that Midsommar was usually just a couple of weeks before the Fourth of July.

However, Thanksgiving was a different matter. It was Nicole's mission to keep the Thanksgiving tradition among her expatriate friends. Planning and executing a turkey or turkeys, and all the side dishes became a daunting task. So did the meaning behind the meal. Nicole was faced with endless questions:

"Why a pumpkin pie? Won't chocolate chip cookies do?"

"The pie is symbolic of gourds served at the first Thanksgiving," Nicole replied.

"Why a turkey? I like your bar-b-qued chicken better."

"The English brought water fowl and a turkey is emblematic of fowl," Nicole replied.

Why is this holiday on a Thursday?"

"Because centuries ago Thursday didn't interfere with the Sunday Puritan church services," Nicole said.

"Why can't we go out?"

"We're celebrating peace with the Indians from over 300 years ago?" Nicole shrugged her shoulders.

The questions and comments were endless, and Nicole's amusement from it all was worth it. On the first Thanksgiving the families shared together, the undersized turkey was picked clean by the kids before the adults could even begin eating. Two sides of boiled corn and potato bake (an Australian tradition) were untouched. The children hated the store-bought pumpkin pie. Nearly two decades later, Thanksgiving is still described as "a work in progress," according to Nicole Nilsson. She hasn't given up on this holiday as it has become another favorite among the families.

While Kathy Searle tried at first to hold onto the cultural traditions of her home country of Australia, she found the traditions of her new friends to be enough enrichment for her family. While there were new holidays, there were also the traditional ones that transcended country of origin, such as Christmas. Always a favorite, the families began to rotate Christmas Day celebrations and gift exchanges each year.

With many adventures, indoors and out, the cadre of friends became broader over time; the village of growing families was becoming close-knit. They seemed to enjoy holidays and happy milestones, not encountering any tragedies beyond the normal childhood mishap. Even then, accidents such as a broken wrist or bicycle crash were viewed as rites of passage resulting in opportunities for an impromptu barbeque and over sympathizing. It was an idyllic life.

Villages happen; they aren't constructed. Without even noticing, a solid village of like-minded people had become established in an urban setting. It wasn't defined by houses grouped together, but rather by hope and love. Each family was committed to each other for the long run, to love each child, and shepherd the needy within the confines of their open arms. There wasn't anything the members of the village wouldn't do for one another. Above all, it was a great place to nurture growing children.

The village was a wonderful place to be, and Nick knew it. Perpetually thrilled with his life, Nick knew his village was special, and never took it for granted. He once said: "Without relationships, one would have nothing."

CHAPTER TWO:
RITES OF PASSAGE

"Those who have lived a worthy life will be rewarded."

– Jewish belief

Taglit is Hebrew for "discovery." Realizing that their life was on a happy trajectory of discovery, Annika and Mitch maintained that Annika's Swedish roots were sacred. Annika wanted to be sure her boys were able to establish their own Swedish roots, maintaining a two-continent balance. Annika wanted them to be familiar and prideful of their dual cultures. Mitch's family lived near Coral Springs, including his mother and many cousins. The only first cousins Nick and Alex had lived in Sweden. Everyone worked hard to cultivate love within the family that knew no distance. Each time they gathered, it was as if they lived around the corner from one another.

Beginning when the boys were just babies, trips to Nora were a highlight for the entire family. One memorable trip was in 2006. Annika smiles as she remembers the excitement her boys felt when it was time to board the airplane for Sweden. Nicholas dreamed about Grandma's Swedish pancakes with fresh lingonberries, a meal he could never get enough of. Nick also mentioned the Nora ice cream, for which there was no match in the United States. Upon landing, the Americans were always met by family. From the first moment he greeted Annika and her family at the airport, Grandpa Nils couldn't stop staring at his bright American grandsons who bore a striking resemblance to his beautiful daughter, whom he had deeply missed. They each had inherited her wide-eye smile, and Mitch's calm and introspective temperament. Nick was blond and blue-eyed, like his mom, and he was a typical husky Swede. He was sweet and tough, all wrapped up into one lovable boy. Grandpa Nils believed that "no" was not in Nick's vocabulary.

While Nils spoke little English, he communicated with his grandsons in age-old ways that required no conversation — through sports and cars. Nils was an avid motorsports spectator and loved to travel to the nearby village of Kumla to watch any type of racing, including motorcycles and go-karts. Grandpa Nils was associated with a team called the Indians and he spent a lot of time there working on their vehicles. Some of his favorite memories were of taking Nick to the races. If they were watching the motorcycles, Nick would get to sit on the seat of the parked motorcycles. If they were watching the go-karts, they sometimes were allowed in the mechanics pit where Nick could look at the go-karts up close. He was in awe of the engines and the inner workings. Nick was intrigued and thrilled at watching motorsports, and Grandfather Nils was equally thrilled watching his grandson's joy.

During the early years, Nick acquired enough Swedish language to understand and converse a little. He became a translator of sorts for his dad and little brother. They frequently confused words and inflection but followed it up with a lot of laughs and smiles, and in the end they "spoke fine" with Grandpa Nils.

This year, the boys were big enough to discover Lake Norasjön. This was the first time they swam outside of the confines of a pool. Both boys had learned to swim before the age of three, and the local Swedes watched in awe as the youngsters dove into the lake at the ages of 6 and 3, much younger than the typical Nora youth. The boys flourished in the lake. When Nick swam away from the shore in a butterfly stroke, people stared as if they had never seen such movement in the water. The boys experienced the taste of mountain water and felt the silt of mountain ash between their toes. It was a clean and carefree existence filled with fun times and cousins who grew so fast that each subsequent trip seemed like meeting new friends.

Grandpa Nils also liked to swim in the lake. Nick and his cousins would swim in any temperature of water out to their favorite platform in the lake that had a slide. Grandpa Nils was the only adult who would swim along. Nils realized the water was freezing but the joy of playing with his grandchildren overrode his senses; they could play for hours. When it came time to return to shore, Grandpa Nils challenged Nick to a race. They dove off the platform together with astonishing athleticism. Nils had perfected the art of the dog paddle; it was difficult to watch and the cold water would quickly overtake Grandpa. His strong arms became tight, and he began to thrash and struggle. Meanwhile, Nick used a perfect freestyle to easily pull ahead. Many who saw these "races" can't remember if Grandpa ever won; he probably didn't.

Following their play in the lake, the entire family enjoyed a campfire. As the sun became weaker, (it never went down) the air became cool. The adults bundled up and huddled together, partially to keep warm, but moreover to share sibling love. Annika adored her sister and brother, and these rare family times were cherished. Meanwhile, the children wandered around wet, teeth chattering, wearing only their swimsuits. Nick begged to go back into the water, oblivious to the temperature. He was easily bribed to stay out of the water with BBQed food. Hot dogs never tasted so good; sometimes Nick consumed two. Annika quickly took this opportunity to clothe her sons, ensuring the day's swimming was over. Nick's favorite part of the evening was eating a sweet treat, usually a piece of Swedish chocolate. Chocolate would typically end up everywhere. At a minimum, it found its way onto his shirt and no doubt, his fingers. If he happened to run his fingers through his hair, chocolate would end up on his forehead as well. As Nick licked his fingers and lips clean, he quietly wondered if he could lick the chocolate off his shirt but decided against it to be polite. As the evening was coming to a close, the tired children began to realize it was cold. Now the entire family huddled by a dwindling campfire, which was slowly smoldering into embers. The group soon boarded a ferry from Lake Norasjön for the short ride back to Nora.

Also, on some afternoons Annika introduced her sons to fika, which is a Swedish tradition of afternoon coffee and desserts shared among neighbors. It's an opportunity to share recent news of interest to the group, which in Sweden is known as polite gossip. Children, while welcome, are not the main focus of fika and they often play together outside or in another part of the house. The host provides coffee. The snacks are homemade; Annika's favorite recipe was sticky cake, a delicious cake similar to a flourless chocolate cake. During one fika, Annika noticed the dessert plates brought into the kitchen were unusually bare. At later gatherings, she noticed Nicholas' little hand reaching for the sweet cookies, pastries, and other delights. He quietly retreated. The only sign later was powdered sugar encircling his mouth like a bad application of lipstick. Fika, too, became a favorite time of day for Nick; no one seemed to notice the interloper.

With one last swim in the lake, one last fika, and one last ice cream cone, Nick reluctantly boarded the airplane for the long ride home to Florida. Exhausted, he slept the whole trip, only waking as the plane landed. Annika had the pleasure of watching her tired boys sleep for many hours, and reflecting upon the trip, she kept visualizing the joy of watching Nick swim in the lake for hours. She and Mitch relished the memories of all the things their boys had discovered on this trip. Their toddlers had become boys. Annika felt, too, that her little swimmer Nick was ready to explore the possibility of becoming a competitive swimmer. But first, he needed to complete Swim America. Upon arriving home, one of the first phone calls Annika made was to enroll Nick in the Swim America program. It began, just about the same time as first grade.

"Liten Simmare" (Swedish for Little Swimmer)

Swim America is one of the most comprehensive developmental swim programs available. It has proven successful in developing many Olympians, but at this point Nick was just happy to see familiar lifeguards and instructors as he entered the pool for his first session since returning from Sweden. His track into the future as a swimmer was formative, but he was in the right place. Nick resumed his progress in the fifth step of the program with freestyle.

That step concentrates on freestyle, introducing Nick to bilateral breathing. Bilateral breathing is when a swimmer breathes on both the right and left sides, a very tricky yet necessary skill that some people never master. Nick learned to trust the process, and more importantly, trust himself in the water. If Nick couldn't master breathing, he could never master swimming. It was just that simple. He mastered breathing as naturally and easily as any child the instructor had ever seen. Nick also smoothed out his kick, making it shorter and faster, and bending his knees less. He learned to lengthen his arms and to discover the rotation of his body in rhythm with his new breathing skills.

When Nick moved on to the next level, he learned how to tread water. This skill is a survival skill, but also serendipitously prepared Nick for the most fundamental skill of water polo, which would be utilized years later. Nick found treading water boring, although he was able to talk which was a welcome diversion while churning away with his powerful little legs. Nick was an expert at talking, and finally, now that he was able to chat with others, time passed quickly.

With little instruction, Nick demonstrated proficiency in diving from the sitting, kneeling, and standing positions. He wanted more than anything to hop up and dive from the starting blocks but knew that would come later. Instructors began encouraging the swimmers in this step to swim farther. Casual timing of laps was introduced to build endurance in freestyle. Nick also worked on his backstroke with correct body position, strong kicks, and quick arm rotation. After perfecting the backstroke, Nick moved on to what would become one of his favorite strokes — butterfly.

While Nick had always enjoyed butterfly, especially in lakes, he never had formal training for this stroke until this step. Nick would soon learn and master the timing of the butterfly stroke. Legal butterfly must have two visible kicks with one arm pull. Breathing should occur every other stroke. Butterfly to Nick was like double the freestyle. He had to move both his arms and both his legs just like the freestyle motion, but all together and all at once. With lots of practice and guidance, Nick's powerful little body fully engaged in the rhythm and beauty of this stroke. Nick also incorporated fundamental technique corrections, such as tempering the strength of his right arm which dominated his left, and reducing the bend in his knees. His instructors had rarely seen such strength and ability in a young boy. Nick developed a picture-perfect stroke. Strangers continued to stop and stare. With the mastery of butterfly, Nick moved up to the next level.

This jump was a bit of a challenge and was dedicated to breaststroke, which happened to be Annika's favorite stroke. Hours were spent on Nick's kick: "Take your feet up, out together, much like a frog," Annika would instruct Nick from the bleachers where she was watching. "Just like a frog." Nick practiced this both in the water and on the pool deck hanging over the edge of the pool. Sometimes he even dreamed about his frog kick while asleep. Next, Nick worked on timing, which is a combination of four mechanical steps: pull the arms, breathe by lifting your head, kick, and glide.

Breaststroke has several nuances that make the swimmer's stroke legal. One such rule is to touch the wall with two hands. Another is to finish the kick with both feet together. Failure to follow these and numerous other rules could result in disqualification in competition. Some say this stroke has the most rules of any stroke. When Nick learned all of them, he was nearly finished with developmental swimming, and could finally see the end in sight. Only two steps stood between Nick and the ability to join the Coral Springs Swim Club.

First he learned fundamental competitive rules, such as the meaning of a false start, and how not to glide on your stomach while performing a backstroke flip turn. He finally learned how to use the starting blocks and how to dive into the pool to start a race. Nick was also taught how to use the powerful underwater dolphin kick legally in competition. The dolphin kick is where the swimmer kicks with both legs together under water upon starting a race and upon turning at the walls. This feature was added to competitive swimming about the time Nick was born. It forever changed the landscape of swimming competition, becoming the hidden weapon that separated champions from others because it added speed and efficiency to a swimmer's race. Luckily, even at a young age, Nick was strong and had exceptional cardiovascular strength to master this kick.

Nick was now ready to move on to the final step, where he was taught techniques to gain endurance and fine-tune his strokes. Nick was taught the basics of becoming a competitive swimmer through the use of kick boards, pull buoys, and paddles. Kick boards disable the arms to strengthen the legs. Pull boys immobilize the legs to strengthen the arms. Paddles are attached to the hands to provide for technique perfection and to also further develop strength. To complete the program, Nick needed to demonstrate proficiency in a variety of races. He did so with ease during sizzler competitions.

Sizzler races, held each Friday, were designed to be friendly competitions which focused upon form rather than performance. The clock didn't matter. The afternoons were usually humid, preceded by midday rain. As parents gathered in the bleachers, weary from work and other demands, the sunny days seemed endless but excitement would soon fill the air. When he could, Mitch would come watch his son swim. Mitch had a demanding job that allowed little flexibility with his schedule. Annika sometimes had to trade shifts with a nursing colleague to make it but was usually present to see Nick swim. Unbeknownst to both mother and son, in these early stages, Annika was forming a healthful ritual with Nick. This ritual meant that he always knew she would be there, and that she carefully supported him in preparing to swim. This included making a nutritious meal, checking his gear bag, and rechecking his gear bag. Lastly, and by far most importantly, Annika talked with Nick and prepared him mentally for the day ahead. Annika was Nick's steadfast fan from the beginning to the end of the swim meet.

As former Olympian Summer Sanders wrote in her book, *Champions are Raised not Born*, "My mom made it her job to keep things not too overwhelming, not too pressured, not too daunting, she made it her job to keep it fun. She kept the fright out of failure. The one thing Olympians have in common is parents who never pushed." Annika and Mitch believed Nick was always a winner whether he was wet or dry. They would watch as the instructors eagerly viewed the student's progress on stroke technique and rudimentary competitive skills such as starts and turns. They were looking for signs that the swimmers were ready to compete in formal swim meets with proper form without regard to times.

When Nick appeared at the starting blocks, he brought both form and performance. His posture exuded confidence. His approach to his competitors was one of friendliness. As the races began, Nick was all business. His strokes were natural. He had speed, and he had mastered most of the fundamentals of competition, including the dolphin kick and legal turns. By age 7, Nick outgrew sizzler competitions and advanced to the swim team.

Alongside Nick in his swimming progression was his first and best friend, Leif. Leif enjoyed swimming but not to the extent that Nick did. Leif completed the Swim America program but also played other sports, such as soccer. Nick enjoyed other sports, too, but each of the boys decided to chase their sporting passions. While these were not the same, their friendship did not change.

From a "liten simmare" (little swimmer), Nick had completed the rite of passage to "stor fisk" (big fish).

Testing the Fabric of the Village

Tragedy would first test the fabric of the modern village in 2009. In August 2009, a family with three children lost their young daughter in an accident in the family pool. Nicole remembers picking up the phone that day to hear her close friend on the other end, hysterical. In the ensuing week, Nicole assumed a leadership role within the community, greeting visitors at the hospital, and interacting with friends, neighbors, and parishioners. She also got a taste of dealing with the media. Nicole rested on the uncomfortable bench in the ICU waiting room for several days while the family toiled through the terrible decision to discontinue life support for their young daughter six days after the accident.

The death left many shaken but resulted in organ donations that benefitted at least four others. Through this experience, Nicole's village, who intrinsically knew all along what she was made of, saw her in action. She became the anchor of the village.

Hundreds of mourners attended the service on a sunny, clear and unseasonably cool day in August. Shortly thereafter, a fundraiser was held to benefit a new foundation being established in her memory. Nicole introduced Annika and Kathy to the grieving mother at this event. Annika glanced at her own boys and for an instant was overcome by a flash of terror at the fear of losing one. Her stomach turned and her mind went astray. Annika was able to gather herself and her thoughts wandered elsewhere. From here on, the village opened their arms and incorporated this family. Their tragedy was a village tragedy, and they continue to be embraced.

Meanwhile, Kathy and Brad Searle were enjoying Brad's early retirement. Brad was a smart, determined guy who had the good fortune of spending a lot of time at home with his young children, each under the age of 10. He was a fabulous cook and enjoyed making dinner for his family, sometimes after Ethan's flag football practice. Brad took a businessman's approach to helping Ethan with his homework, showing him how to apply the structure and drive necessary for success. Ethan became a phenomenal student. Mikaela was still a small girl with very little homework, but she enjoyed her father's playfulness and affection. Kathy was the consummate nurturer and believes the combination of her and Brad's parenting made her children "polar opposites."

About the time of the pool accident, Brad Searle was dealing with cancer, but many did not yet know it. Over the next 18 months, he waged a valiant battle but ultimately succumbed to the disease in 2010. Ethan was 11, Mikaela 7. With back-to-back tragedies, the village was shaken. Most of the Searles' extended family lived on another continent, and the village came together to support and comfort the Searles during this time. Kathy said Annika was beside her "all the way, day or night, and supported her through this terrible journey." Kathy became a widow with two young children before she was 40. Her parents and siblings lived in Australia. The village locked arms around Kathy, surrounding the Searle family with love, making sure they continued to be included in all of the holidays and celebrations. Bo and Mitch stepped up and assured Ethan that he had surrogate fathers. Ethan was never without the support of these men and their sons who were his best friends. Annika and Nicole also helped Kathy with some of the more ordinary parental tasks such as making an impromptu dinner, picking up a child or a last-minute item from the grocery store, and other things to sooth the unanticipated single mother.

The village was beginning to learn that as time moved on, children grow, siblings arrive, grandparents age. Some pass on, good things happen, and tragedy strikes. Nothing stays quite the same.

New to parenting yet another boy, Ethan, Mitch and Bo Nilsson decided to charter a fishing boat. They took five boys out to catch "lots of fish." The weather was not idyllic. In fact, it was rough, and Nick was seasick from the moment the boat left the dock until it returned. He laid on the boat deck nearly the whole trip. Meanwhile, at home, the moms were busy preparing side dishes and accoutrements for an expected big grilled fish dinner. Hours later, the moms received a phone call. Their brave fishermen had returned to port with only one small fish, only capable of feeding its captor, Liam Nilsson. Mitch requested that Annika go to the store and buy some fish. Once he touched land, Nick recovered from his seasickness. Thanks to Annika's quick trip to the store, the families had a great grilled fish dinner later that evening. The five disappointed "fisherboys" forgot about their lack of catch by swimming in the Dworets' pool until late in the evening.

As Annika, Nicole, and Kathy looked over at Mitch and Bo, both men were sitting straight up in folding chairs. Their heads were on their hands, elbows on their armrests, each quietly dozing. The women glanced at one another and knew what the others were thinking: "This is the way our village is supposed to be."

The women poured another glass of wine, and the children continued to play in the pool. As a rare layer of the Everglades' fog blanketed the backyard, it complimented the sense of contentment. Nicole heard a loud snore come from Bo. She promptly stood up and called out to her brood: "Night over, game over, time to go home."

CHAPTER THREE
WHAT THE HELL IS WATER?

"There are these two young fish swimming along and they happen to meet an older fish swimming the other way, who nods at them and says, "Morning, boys. How's the water?" And the two young fish swim on for a bit, and then eventually one of them looks over at the other and goes "What the hell is water?"

– David Foster Wallace

It is hard to pinpoint exactly when the Dworet boys became like two little fish unaware that living in water wasn't normal. There was never a "before" in their lives when it came to swimming; the word "always" was used instead. The boys always seemed to be in the water.

The program instructors now called Nick a "future star" at age 7, and it was Coach Jessica Long's job to develop him into a competitive swimmer. Beyond the sizzler races, there would be greater local competitions, known as club meets, for him to enter. Accordingly, Nick's practices became more structured. Sometimes his parents would have to interrupt him in the middle of playing with his friends in his own pool to go to swim practice. Nick wouldn't argue, but would sometimes look forlornly at the fun he was leaving behind. Nick's memory was short when he realized he was going to his secret, even-happier place. Nick would start to loosen his joints and limber up by doing simple stretches. Annika would be sure he had a healthful snack, while Nick scurried about the house to find his favorite practice suit. When he remembered, he cleaned his goggles, carefully using a mixture of baby shampoo and water. He would then recheck his new swim bag to make sure he hadn't forgotten anything. Nick usually ran for the car slightly out of breath and with a big smile as he waited for Annika or Mitch to drive him to practice. The ride to the pool was always fun. Nick was excited, and the conversation usually led him to ask, "What's for dinner?" because Nick was always thinking about food as a reward for the hard work he was going to put into the pool. On the rare cold day, preparing for practice meant packing additional clothes and shoes. The warmth of Florida is a luxury for swimmers who can wear very little to practice, and dress casually afterward, including open-toe sandals. However, cold weather is a swimmer's enemy, and on cold days, Florida swimmers need sweat suits, parkas, and shoes and socks after practice. Nick, like all other Florida children, was unaccustomed to wearing such clothing; his parents did an inventory as he left the house, and an inventory when he got back in the car after practice. Inevitably, an item would be left in the locker room. Nick's parents described returning to the locker room on cold days to find many items left behind.

Mullins Park was a short ride away, and Nick always arrived ready to swim. Annika and Mitch enjoyed watching their boy practice. His 7-year-old freestyle had become refined and more efficient; it was beautiful, in fact. While in the Swim America program, he had learned how to do a flip turn with a dolphin kick; now his job was to perfect it. Flip turns take time to learn. They are a somersault and one-half twist with the goal of pushing off the wall with your feet. After grazing his head on the bottom of the pool and slamming his feet into the wall several times, it clicked, and Nick became consistent with this skill. Nick came to the realization that the push off the wall was another source of speed. He later learned that this would become the foundation of his "breakout," a term used to describe speed generated when pushing off the wall.

Nick favored freestyle the most. However, Annika and Mitch were able to see him breathe easier and easier while doing butterfly, establishing a rhythm that was beautiful. Nick finally felt comfortable face up while doing backstroke and managed to master his breathing so he wouldn't get water up his nose. Coach Jessica also taught him to count the flags overhead to anticipate reaching the wall. This allowed Nick not to turn his head to look. She also taught him how to do a backstroke turn, another version of a flip turn. Nick was demonstrating the skills and aptitude of a much older swimmer.

Saving perhaps the best for last was Nick's breaststroke; he never gave up in his pursuit of improvement. Nick enjoyed laughing at himself, and breaststroke was always a good topic to initiate laughs. Nick used the kickboard to strengthen his kick, and sometimes paddles to refine his pull. The individual medley requires proficiency for all four strokes, and breaststroke was a weakness for many. Over time, Nick became a formidable breaststroker, so much so, that he readily competed in the individual medley.

On special days, stroke clinics would be held at practice. Coaches would provide swimmers individual technical advice. These clinics would focus on the minute details of a swimmer's stroke. Nick would listen intently to the instruction. For example, in freestyle, the angle of fingers upon entry into the water is very important, and then the catch of water with the hand and the pull underneath must align with a swimmer's rotating body to thrust the water backward. Arm motion in freestyle is much like a person using a paddle to propel a canoe; the more efficient the arm stroke is from the pull, the more strength and speed the swimmer generates. Coaches and swimmers work on this aspect of the stroke endlessly throughout a swimmer's career.

The coaches would also look at Nick's finish, where his hand was done pulling, and lastly, his recovery, which is where the hand leaves the water to start all over again. These four basic elements need to be precise for a competitor to excel. Nick was now favoring freestyle and worked tirelessly on his technique. Entry, catch, pull, recovery. Repeat. Entry, catch, pull, recovery. This was his mantra while he analyzed his stroke on the hours, days, and years he spent swimming freestyle.

Nick was happy practicing and competing with his swim team. Practicing four days per week, he moved through the three groups of the Coral Springs Swim Club program at Mullins Park in four years. Nick enjoyed much success in local competitions during this time. With a quick wit and a wide smile, Nick became a favorite among his teammates. He was always cheerful and positive and added an uplifting atmosphere to a difficult, grinding workout. In some ways, swimming went against

Nick's nature because of how much he liked to talk. Nevertheless, he used the long hours of his head being submerged to reflect within and explore his soul. Once he had his head above the water, he was all smiles and as his mother called him, a "chatterbox." His coaches called him a joy. Nick usually was thinking about a joke or anecdote, and his little brain was churning as fast as his body, so he could get to the wall and share it with his coaches and teammates.

While swimming was becoming an all-encompassing sport, Nick dabbled in other sports. There was a time where he expressed interest in soccer, so Annika enrolled him in a youth league. One Saturday morning, Nick had a preliminary swim meet race, followed by a soccer game at noon, and the final swim race in the afternoon. It was an exhausting, overscheduled day of driving and competing. However, it was a sign that Nick needed to make a commitment and decide if swimming is what he wanted.

Going for the Gold and Blue

Nick tried many sports but preferred swimming. As he grew older, he saw Leif, Ethan, and other friends become sports specialists. Nick, too, became exclusively a swimmer by age 12.

The Coral Springs Swim Club program was comprehensive and also formative. While the program was designed to develop competitors, it also focused on the temperament and minds of the swimmers to determine if they had the aptitude and desire to commit to the sport. Swimming is a difficult sport with back-breaking training and deferred gratification. Nick loved to swim but constantly examined his commitment. By the time he was 12, he was in a good space both in the pool and in his head. He moved up to the gold group. The gold group was the highest level offered at Mullins Park; it provided swimmers who had a good foundation in technique with more detailed training. The gold group swam the longest distances in practice and focused upon advanced competitive skills.

In October 2012, Nick achieved his first Junior Olympic qualifying time in the 50-yard freestyle. He was also recognized as the swimmer of the month. In the club newsletter, Nick was described as "a very talented swimmer who has a lot of potential to be a great swimmer with his work ethic in practice and meets."

The accomplishment of qualifying for the Junior Olympics made it official; Nick's level of swimming had evolved to the most competitive level possible for a 12-year-old. This also meant that he was ready to move up to a higher level of training and switch to the "big pool" – the Coral Springs Aquatic Complex. The complex has an Olympic (50 meters) and short-course (25 yards) pool to accommodate all levels of training. It is a busy place, churning out champions from many nations. Former Olympic coach Michael Lohberg, who died in 2011 from a rare blood disorder, was the former Coral Springs Swim Club director. The local and international legend was instrumental in qualifying swimmers for every Olympic Games from 1984 to 2008, including the comeback of Dara Torres. In Nick's early years at Mullins Park, he dreamed of being coached by Lohberg. Lohberg died just before Nick was about to move up.

Still excited about his elevation to the next level, Nick began swimming in the blue group for Coach Matt Jordan. They practiced in the short-course pool most of the time. It was there where he met many lifelong friends. Many described Nick as a strikingly handsome boy with a young swimmer's physique who turned people's heads when he walked on deck. The only person not taking notice was Nick himself. Out of curiosity, those same people often watched him dive into the pool and take his first few strokes, just to capture a glimpse of how his beautiful body moved in the water.

Among his new friends was Alexio Musleh, a boy of Jordanian origin who came to Florida at age 11 because his older sister Lydia was training at the Coral Springs Swim Club. Lydia had hopes of representing Jordan in international competition. By no means was Alexio's swimming an afterthought; he was a formidable young backstroker and a very serious athlete. His family had sacrificed significantly for their children's swimming careers, hoping it would establish their future in college and elsewhere. His parents lived on separate continents, and in several countries, including Greece and France, to financially support their family. This circumstance was not unusual for many of the swimmers at the club. The Musleh children lived and breathed swimming and American academics, all the while guarded by a watchful mother. When Alexio saw Nick in the pool for the first time, he was struck by Nick's raw natural talent, especially at freestyle and butterfly, something he had never seen before. He was further struck by Nick's humility about the gift of talent he had been given, a trait he said Nick exhibited all his life. Alexio was especially drawn to Nick's "beautiful soul, with no malicious energy," and they became instant friends.

Now 12 going on 13, Nick was evolving in his training expertise, yet he still had a lot to learn. Alexio and Coach Matt taught Nick to independently use the clock. In swimming, coaches train by using sets of distances, called repeats. This is when math in school is useful. For example, four lengths of the pool (in a 25-yard pool) is 100 yards. When you do that five times, it is called a set of five one-hundreds, or 5x100s. Then the clock is added. If the coach instructs "on two minutes," the swimmers will repeat four lengths of the pool (100 yards total) every 2 minutes. The athlete's rest is determined by the extra time they have if they swim faster than two minutes for that repeat. The faster one swims, the more rest they get. If they swim slower than the repeat time, the swimmer gets no rest. Most swimming training is based upon this routine — a set of repeats based on time.

Nick's first few tries at repeats were clumsy. He would sprint for his first 100 yards and be rewarded with rest, but then he would have no energy in reserve by the last repeat, barely getting any rest. Nick would be red-faced and panting as the coach and Alexio reminded him about the need to pace himself and understand the purpose of sets; sometimes it was endurance, not speed they were after. Nick soaked it all up. The coach told

Annika that Nick was a quick learner and a joy to coach. The methods and means of the program became rote to him over time, to the point that he was able to help other young swimmers who were newcomers to the blue group.

One newcomer was Guy Bogoslavsky. Like Nick, Guy had dual citizenship — Israel and the United States. Guy preferred America as his home country, although he had extended family and deep roots in Israel. His grandmother, a Holocaust survivor, had immigrated to Israel from Poland. Guy fit in well with Nick and Alexio, and together with one other boy named Gui Hada, they made up a posse that became nearly inseparable. They all fell into a training routine and pushed each other in the pool. When not in the pool, they each dreamed of when they would be returning to the pool. They called themselves the "Circle of Four."

One of the beauties of the sport is that when training partners swim side by side, mile after mile, there is a private, nonverbal language that is created. Nick came to recognize the patterns in his lane mates' strokes, how they pushed off the walls and finished, their breakouts, and their turns. Without speaking — just by observing each other's strokes — they knew when each other was at the top of their game, or struggling, and vice versa. They understood cues of happiness, joy, fatigue, and most importantly, competition and intensity, which continued to build. Because swimmers are perpetually out of breath and cannot speak much, this language bound the four boys like no other kind of communication and became a motivating force for the group and individually. Every boy was vying for success and would achieve it.

A Need for Speed

Nick had a need for speed; his sprinting abilities were unmatched by nearly every other swimmer. Most workouts didn't focus upon sprinting for various reasons, namely because swimmers can't do a lot of sprinting; it is exhausting. Usually, at the end of practice, the four boys would steal away a minute or two to challenge each other to a 25-yard or 50-yard sprint. Winners were often determined by prerace rest and nutrition because swimmers were usually exhausted and famished after practice. While competitive, these sprints were short, sometimes less than 15 seconds of joy. When they took off, all the coach could see were thrashing arms, splashing water, kicking and then the first arm hitting the wall followed by a fist pump. Their breathing was heavy — to the point of impeding their ability to carry on a conversation. All the winner got was bragging rights until the next day, and once he could talk, he let all the others know it. No one kept score, and no one dominated this competition. It wasn't about winning, it was about much more — friendship and camaraderie. Alexio described it with a big heart: "We had a passion for one another and wanted to see each other succeed."

After their race, each swimmer would shake hands or hug and pat one another across the lane lines before starting to cool down. Cooling down is the process of lowering one's heart rate by moving slowly and gently. It's also about removing the lactic acid from the muscles. Young swimmers, such as Nick and his friends, often short-circuited cool-downs. When finished, they would use their well-built shoulders to push themselves up and out of the pool where they would pull off their caps and goggles. Sadly, their tactile immersion for the day shared with their fellow "fish" had ended. Even though it seemed like every muscle in their body was exhausted, their return to gravity seemed oddly even more punishing.

While in the locker room drying off, pangs of hunger began building in Nick's stomach. Sometimes he was so hungry that he wasn't sure if he could drag his exhausted body out of the locker room to make it to his next meal. Somehow, he would find his way to the car and greet his mom with as much excited energy as he had when he left, telling her first about his practice, and then asking, "What's for dinner?" Nick would lobby his mom to stop for takeout. However, Annika had usually prepared the healthiest of home-cooked meals, and she usually won the argument.

Nick had a legendary appetite. Every one of Nick's friends, except for Guy, have said that Nick would definitely beat them at the dinner table. Guy maintained that he could tie or even beat Nick at "eating" on occasion. Kyle Oliver, another club friend, called Nick a "bear in a trash can" when he spotted a closed pantry door. When Nick would visit Oliver's (better known by his last name than his first) house he would invariably clean out the pantry of snacks, such as crackers, potato chips, cookies and popcorn. Of course, Oliver ate along with him. Likewise, Nick was known to scour his own mom's pantry on a regular basis. Swimming made Nick into a caloric furnace. When pizza was ordered at the Dworets, they planned for one piece each and then for Nick to eat the rest, or even sometimes gave in and ordered him an entire pie. Hunger could wake Nick late at night, and he would consume takeout leftovers that his parents and brother Alex had intended to eat the next day. In other words, the refrigerator looked like a version of scorched earth by morning, where anything worth eating was gone. Of course, all of this food intake was essential fuel for swim practice the next day.

As time went on, the training for swimmers also included dryland exercises. These exercises were done as a group outside of the pool. Nick used dryland as an opportunity to exercise his vocal cords with his endless jokes and anecdotes. While the boys were attempting to strengthen their many muscles, Nick often had the others laughing uncontrollably. While many swimmers dismissed dryland as a waste of time, Nick and his friends made the most of it. They enjoyed having pushup and burpee contests as well as seeing how long they could hold planks. Gamesmanship permitted the boys to start rapping a song to try to get their friends to fail at their planks, thereby winning. The boys also ran for cardiovascular development, all the while discussing what they wanted to eat after practice.

This training group also became focused upon the training tools that would make them successful. Shoulder strength is the single most important physical need at this stage of swimmer development because strong shoulders can ward off injuries as a swimmer ages. Shoulder injuries are the most common injuries in the sport, and the boys knew it. They would experiment with both dryland exercises and drills, and the use of their paddles in practice. Paddles make the hands larger so the feel of the water is more exact, and the volume of water pushed is greater. Paddles are great for developing strength and technique. If a swimmer could point to one tool that created their large, strong, shoulders and arms, they would say it was the paddles.

The boys also tracked their progress, including their splits in practice and in competition. Splits are intermediate times in the middle of a distance swim and can be indicative of one's overall cardiovascular condition. They can help guide a swimmer in determining a pace in competition, or in working harder on certain aspects in practice.

In 2013, 83 swimmers and their family members from the Coral Springs Swim Club decided to support a local race for women's wellness, which included a 5K and a half marathon. The race coincided with the 50th anniversary of the founding of Coral Springs. The race also supported the mother of one of the swimmers, who was battling breast cancer.

Before the race, Nick, Gui, Alexio, and Guy made a pact to stay together and finish together. As legend has it, they finished the 5k together, side by side, but not quite holding hands. However, their times tell a different story. The competitive spirit among the boys arrived sometime during the race. Gui and Alexio battled it out toward the end, finishing within .03 seconds of one another, second and third in their age group, respectively. They then walked backward a bit and waited for the other two boys and all four crossed the line together. That same day, Mitch Dworet ran the half marathon in under two hours, finishing 14th in his age group.

By now, Bruno Darzi had become the new national team coach of the Coral Springs Swim Club. Also an accomplished swimmer and Olympic coach, his leadership brought much hope for the hundreds of swimmers he was guiding. The program was filled with a positive vibe, and it seemed like anything was possible for Nick and all the other young swimmers in Coral Springs. Nick could hardly wait to move up to the national team.

New to Blue

Nick soon was moved onto the blue group, a change which was positive in several ways. Coach Matt was refreshing and enthusiastic and related well to his swimmers. In return, Nick's desire to please Coach Matt was unrelenting. In practice, each repeat was swum like it was a championship race, and in swim meets, high expectations and excitement filled the atmosphere. In Nick's first meet as a blue group swimmer, he was unseeded in the 100-yard free. Unseeded swimmers usually swim in the early heats of an event. Nick dominated the heat, finishing well ahead of some of the other swimmers. When he touched the wall, he excitedly looked at his coach, and with a big grin, said, "Matt, how did I do?" Nick's voice echoed off the cement walls of the pool area and across the aquatic center. Coach Matt looked over and said, "Good swim." Nick used his arms to push himself out of the pool, as his fellow heat swimmers finished. All Nick wanted to do was please his coach. Meanwhile, Nick was unaware of how the rest of the heat had swum. This public conversation, which was meant to be private, was loud enough for his clobbered competitors and other spectators to hear. Annika and Mitch and many of the other parents shared wide-eyed grins at this precious exchange. There were many coaches seated around the pool who looked up from their clipboards recognizing this cute, innocent faux pas. Some broke into a sentimental smile; likely reminding them of countless other moments just like this one, over years past. Perhaps long ago they, too, had done this exact thing; most swimmers have. The coaches went back to their clipboards and nothing more was said.

The Circle of Four continued to train together, compete together and enjoy each other's company. Guy, Alexio and Gui looked forward each day to being greeted by Nick who inevitably had a goofy joke to start the workout off right. There were regular swim meets throughout South Florida; the boys grew and worked hard. Each became known to their competitors and experienced a respectable level of success in swimming.

Near the end of one local swim meet, Nick met a girl named Joymarie. They were strangers, and he startled her as she was fretting over a difficult race ahead. Because it was near the end of the meet and most of her team had left, there were very few spectators in the stands. Despite Joymarie being a member of an opposing team, Nick decided to stay behind and watch her swim. He told her, "Pain is temporary, regret is forever." While she swam the 200 IM, Joymarie said it seemed like Nick was the only person cheering. Nick yelled: "Go, blonde girl!" while walking up and down along the pool deck for the entire race. He called her "blonde girl" because he didn't remember her name. By Joymarie's account, she was "last, by a lot," but she conveyed that Nick didn't even notice. Afterward, Nick walked Joymarie to her towel and swim bag, and stood by while she packed up to go home. He opened a small bag of cookies and asked if she would like an Oreo. Holding the cookie by the edges, Nick gently placed the Oreo in the palm of her hand. Joymarie was intrigued that the results of the swim were the furthest thing from Nick's mind. She realized she had just met a very special person. "Nick was always positive," she said. They became fast friends.

Just like the chance meeting of Joymarie, the Circle of Four continued to accumulate stories of making new friends, competition, and camaraderie as they swam across the state. More than anything, they yearned to move through the blue, senior 2, and senior 1 training groups up to the national training group at the Coral Springs Swim Club. Together.

For, without friendship, "what the hell is water?"

CHAPTER FOUR:
SIMMERING

"It's not that us swimmers don't have a life, we just have a different meaning of life."

– Unknown

In autumn, people come from far and near to Florida to watch the great migration of large schools of fish, such as mullet. Amazingly, some of these schools are miles long. They are surrounded and compressed by predator fish such as tarpon, sharks, and barracuda, to the point that the ocean turns various hues of purple, with flashes of silver. The sea looks like a giant pot about to simmer. Frantic fish jump to escape their prey or find space. Squeezed together out of an instinct of fear of the unknown, this is how mullet protect one another. This is how they survive.

Since meeting in the blue group and moving up to the senior 2 group, the Circle of Four swimmers became closer; they vowed to stay together just like a school of mullet fish. They were training in a program that was beginning to simmer in its own way, burdened by a troubling flux.

A swimming spotlight had shined upon Coral Springs for many years now. In 2008, five-time Olympian Dara Torres, finished her 26-year career, training for her last Olympics at the Coral Springs Aquatic Center. It is there where swimmers could catch a glimpse of Torres and other Olympic hopefuls training in an area reserved for the elite. Swimmers would gather at a safe distance from the pool and whisper among themselves, noticing particular nuances of Torres' technique and her training style. Now 41, Dara followed an unorthodox training program designed to prepare her for sprint distances only. Torres was a six-foot tall, tanned athlete with long sinewy muscles, and not an ounce of body fat. One would never surmise that she had recently given birth, except when they saw her greet her cute infant daughter after practice. Swimmers watched her intently, all the while dreaming that they one day would take her place. Torres made the Olympic dream tangible for any swimmer who watched. Whether Torres was training, or just playing with her daughter at a community pool, when Nick caught a rare glimpse of her he watched her as much as he could.

South Florida is a hotbed for swimming. Gifted athletes, coaches, and trainers flock there to seek the best programs. With many options, and the proven success of the Coral Springs program, athletes from all over the world would come there to train. The pressure to maintain Coral Springs as an international center of excellence for swimming was burdensome. There were many new faces at practice — swimmers and coaches alike. The program was growing and expanding but also losing focus and becoming adrift. There seemed to be unexplained turnover among the accomplished team of coaches, leaving parents and swimmers with unanswered questions and uncertainty. Swimmers would arrive at practice not knowing who would be training them that day. A new coach might be gone again within months, without any notice; they would just disappear overnight.

Consistent coaching is essential to the development of champions and more importantly for the development of a swimmer's mental game. Without consistent coaching, performance will wane. Olympian Summer Sanders described the coach-swimmer relationship as crucial, likening the coach to a third parent in a swimmer's life. Nick, who was always coachable, was looking forward to establishing a lasting relationship with the national team coach. Understandably, he wanted to move up to the national team as soon as possible.

By now, the Circle of Four was in the senior 2 group. Each swimmer in this group was serious and on the crux of moving to the senior 1 group, and then on to the national training group. Day by day, and hour by hour, they swam their hearts out guided by the black line on the bottom of the pool, dreaming of training just a few lanes over with the coveted national training group. That occupied Nick's thoughts. He had yet to connect with the future coach, which seemed confusing. Nick was motivated to continue to perform well physically, but the situation began to wear on his mind. He had been very successful in the 11-12 age group, but now that he had turned 13, he was going to discover the most challenging age group of all.

Aging Up

The 13-14 age group is challenging because the boys are growing and developing at different rates. In appearance, there is a tremendous variance among competitors; while some appear physically like small boys, others look like young men due to growth spurts and intensive training. As of July 2013, Nick was four months past his 13th birthday and although he was physically still a boy, he had qualified for four events in the Florida Gold Coast Long Course Junior Olympics. This was a remarkable accomplishment.

Nick got his first taste of competitive gear for this meet. Annika and Mitch, who were equally or more excited than their son by his Junior Olympic qualifying, decided it was time to invest in Nick's first competition jammers. Jammers can cost up to $400 and are designed to provide less resistance in the water than human skin, maximizing speed. First emerging in the sport the year Nick was born, jammers use compressive material and sleek seams; some designers have actually applied aeronautical concepts to the water. As a result, these swimsuits quash any sense of modesty incorporating a highly engineered tight fit that sometimes required two people to assist the swimmer in putting them on. Knowing the advantage jammers provided, Nick was ecstatic to have his first black pair. He had a blue team cap and blue mirrored goggles so that competitors could not see through to his intense blue eyes. When all dressed and ready to race, he looked like a formidable, scary competitor, even though he himself was not aware of it.

By this time, Nick's habit of shaking hands and expressing praise across the lane lines had spilled over to formal competition. At most meets, Nick approached the starting blocks with a wide smile and genuine friendliness. He greeted his competitors on either side, shook their hands, and wished them "good luck" in the race. As they stepped up to the starting blocks, his competitors were taken aback by Nick's friendliness and appeared shocked. Some were seen shaking their heads. And, after the race, sometimes out of breath and regardless of the results, Nick shook hands with as many competitors as he could, congratulating them. In this way, Nick left a lasting memory. Who was that guy?

Nick posted a solid Junior Olympic performance, especially in the 50- and 100-meter free events. In the 50-meter free, where winners are determined by one one-hundredths of a second (.01), Nick placed 39th out of 66 entrants in the preliminary heats. He was the ninth-fastest 13-year-old. The rest of the finishers faster than Nick were age 14. He also swam his personal best time of 28.42, dropping .96 of a second. Only one other 14-year-old swimmer from his club beat him. Had Nick swum 1.25 seconds faster, he would have been in the finals; that's how close the 50-meter free was. Sometimes it can be a race of less than 30 seconds that demonstrates greatness; the coach just needs to watch for it. Nick had swum a great race. Nick was still waiting to connect with the national team coach and was not able to discuss this performance with him. This left Nick wondering: *Did the coach watch? What did he think? Did he have any ideas for improvement?*

Being left in the position of wondering was unsettling for Nick; it silently and slowly began to wear on his soul. Nick, however, vowed to remedy the situation and to trust the process. Surely, a coach this successful knows any one swimmer could amplify his name as a coach; this is how reputations are built and maintained. Nick wanted to be this swimmer.

At the same meet, Nick dropped two seconds in the 100-meter free, which is a tremendous improvement. For a race of that length, it would be like dropping an hour from a day. He placed in the middle of the field; there were 15 13-year-olds who were faster than Nick. Nick was fourth among his teammates, two of whom were one year older. Nick left these Junior Olympics enthused and inspired to work hard for the next year with a new coach, Chris Jackson. He was expecting to grow as he turned age 14, which certainly was an advantage in this competitive age group. Nick's best chances for physical growth lay ahead over the next year, growth that potentially could allow Nick to dominate the younger and less mature swimmers.

After the Junior Olympics

Following the Junior Olympics, the Dworets departed for Sweden, where they enjoyed a shorter than usual trip with their family. Nick still raced Grandpa Nils, but Nils never gave up, as they both took a dive into the cold water of Lake Norasjön. The enjoyment Nick experienced swimming from the platform seemed to quell any simmering doubt or angst about the sport he had left behind in Coral Springs.

Nick's cousins had grown up a bit, and he enjoyed hanging out with them in a teenage way. Through his now more mature eyes, Nick observed that Nora was so unlike Coral Springs. It was a small, charming old town that provided fun for Nick and his cousins to explore on foot, all the while sharing music and food. As they wandered the cobblestoned streets, the aroma of fresh-baked pastries filled the air. Nick inspired his cousins Jocke, Daniel, Ida, and Elin to like some of his favorite rap music; they inspired him, although it didn't take much urging, to snack at the local bakeries and creameries. The cousins rarely had enough money for all of the snacks Nick wanted to buy.

The best time the cousins had together was at their grandparents' house where they played cards and a game called kubb. Kubb is a combination of bowling and horseshoes played outdoors on the lawn. The objective is to knock over wooden blocks by throwing wooden batons at them. Nick liked kubb because it was a variation of all of the outdoor throwing games that he had played in America. But he mostly liked to play because he liked to compete. Elin and Ida said, "Nick liked to win, and he always won." Maybe the older cousins let him win? Nonetheless, what the family enjoyed most was the home filled with endless laughs. Rarely did the evenings become dark in Sweden, and summer nights became known as "endless sun" by the American visitors. The family would play kubb until the temperature became uncomfortably cool. Then they would move inside and huddle together to play cards. One by one, as the children nodded off, their parents urged them to go to bed. The adults later retired to their own bedrooms, and the large family slept until they were awoken by the aroma of Grandmother's cooking.

When the Dworets returned from Sweden, Nick started eighth grade and resumed club swimming at Coral Springs. The tenor of his training group had changed. Some members had left and new swimmers had joined. Alexio had just returned from Greece, but there were questions about how long he would remain. The Circle of Four was still intact for now, but their attitudes were shifting; there remained a low simmer in and around everyone. Coach Chris was still there, though, and that made the group happy. He was their mainstay and drove them harder than ever.

Coach Chris had his heart wrapped up in the club. In 1991, as a standout junior swimmer, he was one of three hand-picked local age-group swimmers to be the foundation of coach Michael Lohberg's new national team. As a 14-year-old, Chris had recorded three Junior Olympic champion titles. He continued swimming competitively until adulthood. Upon completing his swimming career, Chris stayed on with Lohberg, to become a coach himself, assisting with the development of swimmers of varying levels. However, Chris' heart was forever broken after the death of Lohberg, who was his third parent, mentor and idol. Chris tried to minimize his pain with enthusiasm for his swimmers and at this stage in his coaching career, he genuinely enjoyed the senior 1-level swimmers. It was a challenging and rewarding calling.

Nick trained hard and competed at least once per month in area swim meets. While still young in his age group, he continued to improve his times while he grew physically and mentally. A top-10 finish was not unusual now for Nick, even when swimming against 14-year-olds. He was proud, yet humble, about his performances. But something was missing for Nick. That something was not only in the water, it was on the pool deck. It was a malaise that was pervasive among the team. But Nick, with the support of his parents, applied his positive attitude and proceeded to move forward.

In early March 2014, two weeks before Nick's 14th birthday, he competed in the short course Junior Olympics. Nick was now in the middle of his age group. and A recent growth spurt and continued hard work had paid off. Nick's best event was the 50-yard free where he was the 13th seed out of 61 swimmers. Nick qualified for the finals. He swam in Lane 1 in the finals and placed eighth. Lane 1 is a disadvantage because it is next to the wall where water splashes against the gutter and the backwash can slow a swimmer down. Nonetheless, just one second separated him from the winner. In each of his other five events, Nick placed well.

Nick also swam the 500-yard free, which is a counterintuitive event for a sprinter, not to mention a long, uncomfortable race for any swimmer. The 500 requires strategy and pacing. Swimming this race at the Junior Olympics was a mature, developmental move for Nick. He swam a smart race in 5:03.06. The five-minute barrier is a bell weather for distance freestylers. The goal is to break one minute for each of the one hundreds in the race. Few competitors are able to meet this goal. In fact, no 13-year-old at this Junior Olympics broke five minutes. Out of a field of 54 swimmers, Nick finished 15th and was the third among 13-year-olds. Nick was garnering the notice of many local coaches for his remarkable speed and because he was becoming a more complete competitor at different distances. Nick was also performing well in strokes other than freestyle, all at an unusually young age.

But the real highlight of this Junior Olympics was when the Circle of Four swam the 200-free relay together. Starting out, they were seeded

10th. Alexio was the lead swimmer, followed by Nick, Guy, and then Gui as the anchor. Careful not to enter the water or otherwise disqualify Gui after he finished, Nick, Guy, and Alexio hugged each other, jumping up and down and celebrating their unexpected success, an eighth-place finish. They pulled the diminutive Gui straight up and out of the water by his hands and continued their celebration behind the starting blocks. Competition in the 200-free relay is especially fierce, and eighth place was a major accomplishment, even more meaningful because of their friendships.

As the boys returned to the stands, their excited parents joined them. Coach Chris was there to congratulate them. Each boy knew this would be a very special medal, like no other, and they settled down with a smile of contentment. As they tried to calm the adrenaline moving through their bodies and headed to cool down, the boys continued to smile and look at each other. After leaving the cool-down pool they still couldn't believe it. The Circle of Four had accomplished this together.

Mental and Physical Fatigue

Following the short course Junior Olympics, Nick returned to training and was surprised to find that his unsettling feeling about swimming, otherwise deemed a "simmer," was also felt by his friends. The Circle of Four were simmering together like mullet fish. Gui and Guy chose to leave for other programs, while Alexio, who was perpetually living between Greece, France and the United States, was unsure of how long he would stay in Coral Springs. Nick was crushed. He became unable to see why he was swimming. Even though deep inside he knew he couldn't live without swimming, he also was confused by the lack of structure within the program. Nick had relied upon inner drive for so long, yet his tank was running low.

One morning, Nick awoke with an earache. Thinking nothing of it, he went to practice where he missed his three friends, a situation which led him to work even harder than normal, if that were possible. Nick was a zero-sum-game swimmer in practice. He never slacked and never swam slow. Fast and faster were his only options. Following this practice, his ear began to throb. He recalled a circular conversation with his mom about wearing a cap at practice, and how he stubbornly told her that caps caused ear infections, while she maintained they did not. Now he was going to have to tell her she was right about caps protecting the ears. As he returned home that evening, exhausted beyond belief, he told his parents about his earache. Now it was getting bad. Annika treated the ear as any nurse would. Nick officially had joined the swimmer's ear club.

Nick continually had a circular conversation with his mom, a nurse, about the value of wearing caps in practice. He now admitted that she might be right; wearing a cap in practice just may help "a little" to safeguard his ears.

On top of swimmer's ear, Nick had a spell of other minor illnesses that kept him out of practice. He missed his friends, which caused mental fatigue. All of these circumstances disrupted his training. Nick's commitment to swimming slipped. But he stayed on through the July 2014 long course Junior Olympics.

Timing wise, this event was Nick's best opportunity to compete at the top of his age group. He felt a lot of pressure to place in the multiple events for which he had qualified. Nick had trained now for nearly 18 months, and hypothetically was prepared to compete. But Nick was not at the top of his mental or physical game; he failed to place in any of his events. His disappointing performance was due to a more serious reason. A malaise had overcome him. As hard as he tried to shake it off, he was feeling he needed a change.

Coach Chris noticed Nick's struggles and found time to talk him through this period. Chris was tough but empathized with Nick. He had been in the same position years ago. Chris was invested in Nick, training him over the long run, and had been personally committed to Nick's success. During Nick's performance at this meet, Chris had this advice for

Mitch and Annika: "I know Nick has had setbacks this year, and hasn't had stellar health, however he shouldn't give up. His talent has gotten him through this competition. While Nick hasn't done as well as he wanted to, he has unusual raw talent. You cannot train talent, and not every kid has it. Nick is special; he has potential to go very far in this sport."

Mitch and Annika were relieved to hear what they intuitively knew: All of the hours of toil and work were worth it. The validation by Nick's coach was comforting.

As Nick completed his preliminary heat in his last event, the 100-meter free, he placed ninth — one place shy of making the finals. Coach Chris, realizing Nick was an alternate for the finals, encouraged Nick to return later that evening in case there was a scratch, which would provide him the opportunity to swim. However, Nick was a no-show. In fact, he had told his parents that he was done with the sport.

New Friends

Not only did Nick quit the Coral Springs Swim Club, he declared that his competitive swimming days were behind him. Now that he didn't have to work out, he could sleep in late and had a lot of time on his hands. Summer seemed to be endless, and he and his old friend Leif often got together in the late afternoons to walk to familiar places such as Mullins Park. Along the way, they met a new group of boys and quickly became friends. Some of these boys smoked and dressed in dark clothing; others had dropped out of high school. Together, they listened to rap music and had little or no parental supervision. Many came from broken families. Few had plans for the future. From time to time, they also had a lot of money, confusing yet alluring to Nick.

Nick was easily influenced by these charismatic boys and for the first time in his life, he learned what partying meant. Nick and Leif liked being accepted by this group which seemed to push the boundaries with a carefree attitude about life. They had a flair for fashion; in fact, one wanted to be a fashion designer. He introduced Nick to flashy and expensive clothing labels such as Versace and distributors of high fashion such as Supreme. The more Nick and Leif liked their new friends, the less their parents liked their new friends.

The boys were curious about Nick's relationship with rapper HiRez, who was Nick's second cousin Jessie, reinvented. As Jessie chased his adult dreams, the cousins grew apart. Nick, though, was always proud of Jessie's lyrics and his commercial success.

One of Nick's favorite songs was HiRez's "Smiling." Nick knew the chorus by heart:

If I found a way
To be happy everyday
If you could just see my face
Y'all would see I'm smiling
The clouds are never grey
If only there was a place
If you could just see my face
Then y'all would see I'm smiling

Scan this code with your camera to view Hi-Rez performing "Smiling."

This chorus seemed to describe Nick completely. For Nick, the pressure of swimming was gone, and the excitement of high school was just around the corner.

In the hopes that Nick would settle down, Annika bought him more games for his Xbox. When not with his friends in person, he would spend hours playing video games and communicating online with people. Annika and Mitch didn't quite understand how these games worked, but Nick became infatuated, isolated in his dark room. This was quite a contrast from their happy swimmer who just months prior was often seen floating in their backyard pool listening to music. The Xbox created a cocoon that surrounded Nick to the exclusion of all others; he liked it that way. His family did not.

One of Nick's most favorite games was called "Black Ops Zombie." He liked to play it with his old pal Kyle Oliver. They always joked with one another that neither had ever made it past Round 17, before perishing at the hands of a zombie. Each game took about 20 minutes, and they routinely played a couple of games when they met up at one of their homes. When Nick came out from his room it was to eat or go out with his friends. There was no mention of swimming, working out, or his old competitor life. It was difficult for Annika to drive by the aquatic center and see the beautiful turquoise pool, where on most afternoons her boy used to emerge, dry himself off, and greet her with endorphin-fueled happiness.

Now, Nick's family did not know who he was. With drastic changes in such a short time, the summer of 2014 proved to be a new world for the Dworets. One hot and humid summer weekend before school was to begin, Annika, Mitch, and Kathy Searle decided to escape the above 90-degree heat of inland Coral Springs and take their families to Deerfield Beach. Deerfield, often a favorite haunt of both families, usually created excitement for all the children. This day, Annika had to pry Nick away from his Xbox. Under protest, he reluctantly climbed into the car only after being assured that Ethan was coming along, too. Annika and Mitch promised Nick a pizza in the later afternoon, as a reward for getting out of the house. Upon arriving at the beach, Annika and Kathy discovered that both of their sons had only worn jeans! Nick usually was the first boy out of the car and into the ocean. But this day an entirely different boy had appeared. Nick slowly sauntered to the sand uninterested in his surroundings. He begged Annika and Mitch to go home. Nick and Ethan began to perspire profusely yet refused to take their shirts off. Surrounded by the silence of earphone-decked, fully clothed, hot teenagers who obviously couldn't go into the water, the entire group felt uncomfortable. It was a short trip.

When the first day of high school approached, Annika glanced into Nick's darkened bedroom at the 200-free-relay medal hanging behind his bed. For a moment, she relived that joyous moment at the Junior Olympics and wondered about the other three boys. She missed Alexio, Guy, and Gui, and the other wholesome children from the Coral Springs Swim Club. Annika silently thought to herself, "Perhaps high school will bring my swimmer back."

CHAPTER FIVE: TREADING WATER

"At one time or another in life most people can describe their lives as 'treading water.' Many tread against fear of realizing they are not the people they should be, or the fear of becoming who they are. As they thrash against their fluid thoughts, deep down inside they know they will lose the fight..."

– Anonymous

One day, it seemed like the rap music suddenly stopped, and so did the fun. It was time for high school. Unfortunately, the mindset of Nick and his friends was of treading lazily through life with their chins barely above water, subsisting and nothing more. They seemed happy this way. They took no advantage of the opportunities of summer, and were not progressing, just continuing to do the same things. They had no jobs, no money, and no aspirations. The tight group of boys needed little; just the basics such, as food and shelter. They hung out a lot together. Most of the boys with seemingly few advantages in life felt slighted. With absent or uninterested parents, they had no desire to go to school; it was the furthest thing from their minds. As the summer crept on, the boys shared their anxiety, excitement, and trepidation about going to high school. Nick's high school, Marjory Stoneman Douglas, was located a few miles north of Nick's house. Many of his friends were attending other schools nearby. They seemed to be going to school to expand their teenage business interests. Their summer routine of meeting up with friends, hanging out and doing what some groups of boys do—vaping, taking edibles, etc.—was continuing regardless of school. Of course, they enjoyed cutting class to partake in these activities. Education had little purpose in these boys' lives, and they believed everyone should feel the same way. At first, Nick was sheltered from a lot of what they did, but the boys loved being with this new, bright, positive friend. They were always happy when Nick appeared and couldn't get enough of him. The group had a need to hold Nick close and make certain that their convert would become an expert at ignoring school.

Marjory Stoneman Douglas is tucked in a northwestern corner of Broward County. It's a stone's throw from the Florida Everglades, an ideal location to honor its namesake. A legendary Floridian, Marjory Stoneman Douglas was a famous environmentalist who championed Everglades conservation for most of her life. In 1947, she authored "The Everglades: River of Grass." The book served as a template for Douglas' successful one-person crusade to have the Everglades recognized as a national park rather than a swamp. The book has been assigned in literature classes at the school bearing her name.

The high school opened in 1990, the year of Douglas' 100th birthday (she lived to be 108) and 10 years before Nick's birth. Although blind in her later years, Douglas was told in detail about the beautiful new school built in her honor, framed by the river of grass. She was always a humble woman and believed that the best evidence of her life's work would not be her name on a building (her name is on many buildings in Florida because of her civic contributions), but rather to have the Everglades preserved and made healthy again. The first senior class of Marjory Stoneman Douglas, "MSD" or "Douglas" as it came to be known, graduated in 1992 from this huge, sprawling campus reachable by Interstate 75, one of Florida's largest highways. Enrollment now exceeds 3,300 students of many cultural backgrounds and interests. It is common, especially on game days, to see many students wearing the school colors of burgundy and silver in support of the Eagles sports teams.

On the first day of school in 2014, Nick seemed overwhelmed. Douglas was a big contrast to small, quaint Coral Springs Middle School, from which he had just graduated. He was in awe of the confluence of new students from many middle schools that fed his big, new high school. It was akin to the many small streams originating in Lake Okeechobee to the north, which slowly feeds into the river of grass that becomes the Everglades, glimpses of which he could see from his upper-floor classrooms in the freshman building.

Nick had a choice of high schools and chose Douglas after conferring with his parents. It is well known that Douglas had the better swim program of the two. At this moment, swimming was in the rear-view mirror. Except for committing to recreationally supporting the MSD water polo team, Nick was done with high-level competition. He wanted to explore other hobbies. Among the throngs of students, Nick searched the hallways for his new friends.

When Nick and his friends found each other, their talk was not about academics, but rather the social opportunities the new, big school provided. They had identified lots of pretty girls who could possibly be new girlfriends. This was exciting. At this age, the boys delved in and out of relationships with girls. Girlfriends weren't hard to get, but they were hard to keep. With no ambition to speak of, the common passions of these boys were to hang out and take photographs, in that order. Most girls didn't find this to be too appealing.

Nick and one friend had discovered a common interest in photography. Over time, they developed talent and technique, which was impressive way beyond their years and rudimentary equipment. In particular, their use of light was complex, and of a professional caliber. Annika and Mitch realized Nick's passion and purchased a Fujifilm FinePix camera for him. His skills improved as his equipment improved.

Traveling around the local landscape at sunset, the boys captured beautiful images of nature. They sometimes ventured east toward the ocean for shots of the shoreline and other local sites of beauty. Nick's friend had a gift for photographing human emotion in a way that was captivating. He was intrigued by moments of sadness and joy and captured his images with a mature and sympathetic eye. Nick learned this skill from his friend. The boys spent hours together, mostly after school, in curious pursuit of the next perfect shot. All the while, their undone homework remained safely tucked away in their backpacks.

Meanwhile, the Dworet household was in upheaval. Goofing around in the summer was one thing, but inattention to school was another. Since starting high school, Nick was still not Nick, and things were not getting any better. Gone was the sweet, kind, happy young man who rarely entertained a negative thought. Nick had morphed into a defiant rule-breaker. He seemed to have an answer for everything; his parents knew nothing. Unaccustomed to their polite boy talking back, Mitch and Annika began to argue with Nick frequently. He came home late and went out at all hours. Meaningful communication was nonexistent. Nicole, Annika's best friend, had the same frustrations because Leif, her son and one of Nick's best friends, was doing the same thing. At least Nick and Leif were together. Where? Who knew?

Displays of temper were unusual for Nick's parents. However, one evening after learning that Nick was in danger of not passing two classes, Mitch had reached his limit. He entered Nick's bedroom and pulled every cord for every electronic device from the wall. This included the television, computer, Xbox and phone. Mitch's only physical contact was with power cables; all the while Nick was snickering from his bed. Finally, as his parents took inventory of all of the items in their hands, Nick continued to smile and said, "You took the charging cable, but you forgot this," and he handed his Apple phone to Annika. She grabbed it and both parents left the room.

Later, realizing that Nick needed a phone for safety, Annika provided him a phone that had cellular service for emergency dialing only. It had no text or data features. She believed he would carry it with him to school and other places. Annika later learned Nick left the phone at home, not because it lacked data services, but because he didn't want to be seen with an "older model." The affluence of many of the students at MSD was always a subtle pressure upon all the students, including Nick. Cell phones were only one symbol of the pecking order.

Where Was That Nick Dworet?

Marjory Stoneman Douglas is a powerhouse in many sports, especially baseball. A number of MSD students have reached the majors, including three-time All-Star first baseman Anthony Rizzo.

Between class periods, droves of teenagers walk among buildings and classrooms on the sprawling campus. Many of the corridors are tight because they've been designed to shelter students from the frequent rain. In this moving crowd of slamming lockers, backpacks, cell phones, laughter and teasing, the male swimmers stand out. The best way to identify them is through their florescent-tinged hair, an unavoidable byproduct of the hours spent in chlorinated water. Physically, their wide shoulders and chiseled, developed bodies are hard to miss. They are taller than most and go in search of each other like fish seeking their schools. Once together, they would wander the hallways with a sense of kinship and intensity, not usually thinking about girls, or much of anything, besides how to make their team more dominant during the upcoming season.

MSD usually performed well in the South Florida division in both water polo and swimming but fell short when it came time for statewide competition. This was a frustrating circumstance that baffled the swimmers and their coach, Lauren Rubenstein. The swimmers and water polo players at MSD wanted more. They wanted to be on par with the baseball program, and to dominate the state of Florida, not just a part of it. Together, Coach Lauren and the water-based athletes were working toward this goal.

The first week of school, Nick attended freshman orientation where the school clubs had set up informational tables in the cafeteria. This feature of orientation is designed for students to explore activities they may be interested in, connecting them to leaders of the various clubs to bolster participation. Already overwhelmed by the sheer volume of students and the variety of activities and influences at the school, Nick wandered the cafeteria, walking past the debate club, the drama club, and many others. He made pleasant conversation, but the whole process was intimidating. Annika and Mitch also came to freshman orientation, and they noticed that Nick looked out of his element. The photography club was interesting, and he spent some time there, taking a brochure and making a promise to come to the next meeting. This interaction gave Nick the confidence to proceed onward, to look at the other clubs.

At the end of the cafeteria, Geoffrey Roseman, an upper classman, was in charge of the water polo/swimming table. Assisting him was Tristan Celestin, a standout swimmer, and Geoffrey (Geoff) Hayman, captain of the water polo team. The friends had personally taken on the challenge to improve their teams. As the boys were milling around the table, they ignored the pretty girls walking back and forth. They were looking for that unmistakable physique and signature neon greenish-blond hair of incoming freshman swimmers. They had one goal — to improve the water polo and swim teams. These boys needed to catch each and every swimmer; it was time to close the gap and show what MSD water sports were made of.

Nick paused at the table. Geoff and Tristan, in deep conversation, looked up midsentence and stopped talking. Geoff remembers thinking, "This is probably random. Don't jump up and cheer just yet." They knew of Nick, of course. But Tristan was thinking, "If this boy is Nick Dworet, he was not the Nick Dworet I expected."

Nick's body looked soft. Gone was his swimmer's physique of wide shoulders and well-defined biceps. While Floridian swimmers are usually tan, Nick was pale. Gone were his swimmer's core and powerful sprinter look. Instead, Nick's body looked scrawny. His hair was dark and shaved up the sides. His usual bright athletic T-shirts had been replaced by dark jeans and a grungy T-shirt.

Geoff and Tristan had heard that Nick was a freshman at MSD, but they had also heard he had quit swimming. So, they proceeded cautiously.

"I want to play water polo," Nick said.

Wisely, Geoff replied: "If you swim, you would be in better condition to sprint for the water polo team, and that's where we need you. Otherwise, as a freshman, if you don't swim, you probably won't get to play."

The swimming season precedes the water polo season, so Nick and Tristan looked at one another and made small talk. Nick absolutely did not want to swim, and he knew it would be several months before water polo began. Nick paused for a while and hung around the table. Geoff and Tristan talked with other students. When it came time for club day to end, Geoff and Tristan began to pack up their table. They looked up expecting to see Nick, but without a goodbye, he had slipped away. Geoff sighed. "Damn," he said to Tristan. "We missed our opportunity to catch the big fish of our dreams."

Yet, at the same time, the two had a new purpose. The answer to their prayers, Nicholas Dworet, one of the best sprinters around, was on campus. Nick's reputation as a talented swimmer and fierce competitor had long been established in the Florida swimming community. Those who knew him, friends and foes, concurred that his potential had yet to be realized. Nick's calm demeanor and happy temperament had been legendary, so even among opponents he was widely liked. He really had no enemies. Respect followed him everywhere, and the excitement he possibly could bring to the high school swimming program was palpable. But where was that Nick Dworet?

The rumor — that Nick was in the building — spread like a mullet fish being chased through the school of high school swimmers. Tristan decided to close the deal, he needed help from Kyle Jones, another incoming freshman, who despite his status as a standout swimmer, preferred water polo over swimming. Kyle would be the necessary link to sell Nick on the package deal to swim and to play water polo. They decided to team up to hook Nick. Nick was hard to find because he looked like any other high school student. Tristan finally located him walking the hallways between classes. Kyle quickly joined the boys. Their discussion was described as an easy soft sell resulting in Nick joining the MSD swim team. He committed to the team, but reminded Tristan and Kyle that his swimming would be limited to high school swimming only. No club swimming. Nick was going to continue having fun, pursue photography, hang out with his friends. He was going to enjoy the next four years. Life was not going to revolve around the pool.

A Fish of Contradictions

There was celebration back in the swimmers' den, better known as Rubes' classroom. This was the classroom of Coach Lauren. She was a larger-than-life teacher, woman, and surrogate mother to the swimmers. She was a member of the eighth graduating class of Marjory Stoneman Douglas in 2000, and while in college she yearned to return there to teach. She was honored when the offer was extended.

Coach Lauren was a champion swimmer while growing up. At age 4, she became a member of the Coral Springs Swim Club. But the pressure and two-a-day workouts, which began at age 8, proved to be too much, too soon. She burned out early in club swimming but later found her competitive stride in the sport during her high school years. After attending Valencia College and the University of Central Florida, she landed her dream job at MSD and found her true joy in the pool was coaching. Coach Lauren was the rule keeper and culture keeper for swimming and water polo, and sometimes had to coach her students beyond the pool. She intuitively knew this would be the case with Nick.

Although it was a coup for the swimmers to get Nick, he was largely an unknown commodity for Coach Lauren. She found Nick to be a bright, happy, and engaging young man, and she understood the inside stories about his disappointment and burnout with the sport. Even though she was completely satisfied with her short-lived but distinguished swimming career, once Coach Lauren saw Nick swim for the first time, she resolved to help him make his high school outcome different than her own. That is, if he wanted it. But did he? Nick was a fish of contradictions;

not quite saltwater and not quite freshwater, and the coach didn't know if he would sink or swim when she saw him in the pool.

The swimmers and Coach Lauren purposefully put little pressure on their freshman star during his first season. Nick enjoyed the dual meets. They turned out to be small, quaint swim meets where participants would swim a variety of events. Each event would have only one heat of up to eight swimmers, four from each school. Club swimmers usually had a tremendous edge over the nonclub swimmers. But Nick was still conditioned enough to swim at a high level and he was still growing. While not a formal part of the qualifying for state championships, the Broward County Athletic Association (BCAA) holds separate championships before the regional and state championships in Florida.

In the fall of 2014, Nick swam two individual races and two freestyle relays at the BCAA championships. As a freshman, he was competing against some opponents who were three and sometimes four years older than him. Nick accumulated 21 points for his team. He placed seventh in the 200 IM (50 yards of each stroke) out of a field of 28. He placed 15th in the 500-yard free out of a field of 45. Nick's times were not significantly different than his short course Junior Olympic times posted earlier in the year, which meant he hadn't lost much of his core conditioning for the sport.

In the relays, Nick swam with older teammates. He was the leadoff swimmer in the 400-free relay, posting a blistering 52.28 100 split. This relay placed ninth. In the 200-free relay, he swam third with the relay finishing seventh.

Overall, only four Marjory Stoneman Douglas swimmers scored more points than Nick at these BCAA championships. In short, Nick had an unbelievable performance for a freshman. As they packed their happy, excited, and hungry boy in the car, Annika and Mitch hoped their son was back on track. As a way of celebrating Nick's freshman success, the Dworets stopped by the Whole Foods prepared food bar, where the take-out food is priced by the pound. Each family member filled their own small brown cardboard container with favorite foods to be shared later in the food court. Understandably, Nick's container was heaping. At checkout, his helping alone was over $38. Realizing you cannot return prepared food, Annika and Mitch looked at each other and shrugged. Then, they started laughing. As they sat at a table in the food court, Mitch and Annika noticed that Nick's box was empty in an instant; he probably was still hungry.

Nick's first semester of high school was coming to an end. His interim grades were not impressive; he was barely passing. Yet, he seemed satisfied with his academic performance, and not motivated to change. Gradually, he had earned the return of some electronic devices but overall, Nick still was not completely back. Annika and Mitch were seeking a solution. Nothing seemed to work to the degree that Nick's parents had hoped for. However, unbeknownst to everyone, the solution was around the corner and would reveal itself shortly.

Cutting a Deal

With swimming over, Nick was free to cavort with his friends. The party boys had been hanging around the pool some as Nick swam, but now they had a lot more time to get together and to explore photography and other things. It felt liberating for Nick, but burdensome at the same time. Swimming as a freshman had been fun; it had been rewarding, but there was nothing next. Nick was astray; he believed he had no control. At this stage in high school, he didn't yet see a pathway to success, or for that matter, a pathway to anywhere.

During this time, many of his lifelong friends, including Ethan Searle, began putting pressure on Nick to consider changing his ways. Ethan found that Nick's continued partying was becoming a wedge in their friendship. Ethan wanted the old Nick back — the healthy, happy swimmer who had everything going for him. Finally, Ethan initiated the most difficult conversation he had ever had in his young life and told Nick they couldn't be friends if his behavior didn't change. Nick needed to respect his parents and his friends, and to come home at a decent hour. Nick needed to pay attention in class and do his homework. Nick needed to have goals in life, and to be positive about the future. After all, Ethan said, "You have a father and a mother who love you, and every opportunity in life." Ethan doesn't recall if Nick had a response, but he does remember that he didn't give up on Nick.

While Nick was growing up, he had never once considered playing water polo. And so, it was perplexing that going into high school he wanted to play it with a passion. Water polo is like playing football in a pool, and the body contact and physicality is a turn-off for many. Broken facial bones, knocked-out teeth, perpetual nose bleeds, black eyes, and lots of scratches are expected when a person plays water polo. Nick was always so happy competing at swimming that the thought had never crossed the minds of Nick's parents that he would consider water polo. By and large, swimming is an individual sport and water polo is a team sport. But that was exactly what was appealing to Nick about water polo. He wanted to be a part of a team. The lonely swimmer had sought and found his place.

With water polo season just days away, the team was still uncertain if Nick was going to turn up to play. Since the end of swimming season, he had not been seen in the pool. The water polo team was in desperate need of a sprinter, and no one could play that position better than Nick. But Nick was a no-show as the team practiced in anticipation of his arrival.

Geoff went in search of Nick to remind him of their conversation months earlier when Nick was gung-ho to play water polo. Nick now seemed lukewarm. Geoff asked him to try one practice, and carefully defined Nick's scope and role on the team. Then, exercising his authority as captain of the team, Geoff sweetened the pot. Nick was offered the opportunity to sprint only, and to play without practicing, which is normally taboo in high school team sports. In other words, he just had to show up and be the fastest swimmer to the ball and throw it backward to a teammate. Job complete.

Although not fully aware of Nick's conflicts and his struggles during freshman year, Kyle Jones also had a conversation with Nick. The two boys were becoming closer. Kyle felt that the invitation to play water polo was exactly the positive influence and environment Nick needed to bring a sense of order and structure to his life. The power of peer persuasion worked. Nick decided to try it out. Many say it was the first time he had smiled in a while. He seemed relieved.

Although it was a coup for the celebrating water polo players, they now had to reckon with Coach Lauren. Geoff had cut a deal. He wasn't asking but rather explaining the exception. Geoff, a mature and exceptional leader who was not timid, approached Coach Lauren and told her that "Nick would play but not always practice."

Later, when the reality of the deal was exposed, the coach discovered that Nick wouldn't practice at all. All Nick would do was sprint. Coach Lauren was in a quandary. She had never made an exception like this. At the next water polo practice, she stared at the players wondering how a lifelong swimmer who was on the fence to begin with, could be so valuable to the team. Coach Lauren had seen countless swimmers fail at water polo. Reluctantly, she allowed Nick to try water polo.

Everyone, including opponents, knew that Nick's fast-break or sprinting abilities would be superior to all other players in their high school leagues. At first, the conditions of his play were all on Nick's terms, discussed briefly with his parents, and likely the worst-kept secret within his team. Geoff knew that Nick's parents wanted him to focus on his craft, which was swimming, and not obstruct his unrealized dream. However, Nick was a long way from that dream and both boys had gotten what they wanted. Geoff got his sprinter, and Nick found a way back from an unfortunate social environment. Deep down inside, Nick knew he needed water to move forward and escape his circumstances.

New Skills

Now vested in his team's success, Nick knew he needed to quickly develop water polo skills. Nick asked Kyle to help him out. The two boys began to practice dry ball — tossing the water polo ball back and forth outside of the pool. There was no body contact but this drill allowed Nick to develop some of the one-handed catching and throwing skills needed for water polo. In the hot Florida sun, they would sweat puddles on the pool deck throwing the heavy yellow water polo ball back and forth for what seemed like hours. When Kyle wanted to stop, Nick wanted to continue; Nick always felt his dry-ball skills could improve.

When they got enough of dry ball they jumped into the refreshing pool where Nick learned eggbeaters. Eggbeaters are leg movements which both propel and maintain position for the players. Nick's strong quadriceps proved to be great assets for his eggbeaters, even though they were in need of conditioning. The movement of eggbeaters consists of leg motion back and forth and side to side in a churning motion, with little to no use of the arms. The human body is turned into the old-fashioned, hand-turned manual beater like his grandma used to have. Then Nick's mind would wander to Grandma's Swedish pancakes; she would be arriving in two weeks to see him play. Realizing he was daydreaming, Nick got back to honing his new skills. In water polo, eggbeaters are essential for stamina, elevation, and stabilization during play. They look a lot like treading water, but by now Nick was heading in a direction ever so slowly. Without knowing it, he had created just the motion he needed to stop his negative inertia and move on with his life.

Play in water polo begins with a swim-off. Teams are positioned at opposing walls and the referee drops the ball into the middle of the pool. A sprinter from each team swims as fast as he can to get to the ball first, then usually passes the ball to a teammate, and play commences. This was Nick's job as a sprinter.

This first year, Nick always arrived at the ball first and passed it on, winning every single swim-off of the season. Sometimes the mate would pass it back, and Nick would be able to score. Grandpa Nils and Grandmother Birgitta were able to see Nick in one of his games where he scored a goal. It was a highlight of their trip that year. The expectations were simple: swim fast and get to the ball first. Games are divided into quarters, so there were a lot of swim-offs.

At most home water polo games, cheering in the stands was Tristan, a talented swimmer. As Tristan watched Nick, he concluded that he needed a lot of work over the coming summer before his sophomore year to complete Tristan's grand plan. The swim team had big dreams for Nick.

Nick's partying friends also hung around the water polo games, reminding him that there was more to life than swimming. Tristan loved to stare down these boys, hoping they would fade away. "He's our fish now," Tristan would say to himself. With disparate groups of friends, Nick felt as if he were trapped between two continents separated by a foreboding body of water. From time to time, he still hung out with the wrong crowd. Some of the water polo players liked to indulge in eating junk food, engaging in video game marathons or trolling questionable places on the internet. This became an enjoyable contradiction for Nick and his teammates at this formidable time in their new relationships.

Annika and Mitch, however, were not so happy to realize that even the swimmers seemed to stray. One warm evening, Kyle and Nick took off on foot from Nick's house to hang out with the partiers. Kyle was curious about what was so fun about hanging out with these boys. They entered a parking lot and were greeted with a car full of teenagers. Realizing there was not enough room for them in the car, Nick and Kyle walked away. A moment later, the inebriated driver backed his car into a boulder, smashing the entire rear end of the car. As parts of the car showered the pavement, Nick and Kyle were startled and realized they didn't want to be a part of the aftermath of this accident. The two boys broke into a fast walk and then a slow jog. Slightly breathless, they vowed out loud to each other never to hang out with this crowd again. As they turned the last corner onto a familiar cul-de-sac, they ran even faster toward Nick's house.

Like diving into a cold pool, this was a moment that stunned Nick. Nick had turned a monumental corner. The corner was called change. He alone could decide whether to return or not. In this instant, Nick had been shown just what was needed to move on to a healthier order. Would he make the most of this opportunity? Was Nick finished treading water?

Annika and Nicholas Dworet, 2000, in California, where Nick was born.

The young Dworet family, Nick second from left, circa 2005.

Alex Dworet and Nick sharing ice cream together in Nora, Sweden, circa 2008.

The cousins were inseparable when they got together. Elin (left) and Ida Pettersson live in Sweden. This photo is from a visit to Sweden, circa 2008.

Nick finishing his first 5k in 2007

Nick and Alex at Deerfield Beach, circa 2010

Deerfield Beach, 2011, left to right, family friend Riley McCarthy, Alex Dworet, cousin Elin Pettersson, Nick Dworet, cousin Ida Pettersson, and family friend Tyler McCarthy

Family photo, circa 2012

The inseparable Circle of Four swimmers after finishing a 5k in 2013. Left to right, Nicholas Dworet, Guy Bogoslavsky, Alexio Musleh, and Gui Hada. Photo courtesy of Guy Bogoslavsky.

Nick, 13, in his first pair of racing jammers in 2013

Grandmother Birgitta, Nick, and grandfather Nils Persson at a Marjory Stoneman Douglas High School water polo game, spring 2014

The promposal Nick made to Daria to attend her prom, Spring 2016

The showstopping couple, Daria's prom in 2016

Image posted to social media on Valentine's Day 2017 with the caption: "Today is a day not about giving items to each other but showing your love for one another, I am so thankful every single day to have such a wonderful and amazing girlfriend and today is the day to just look back and appreciate that. Appreaciate all the people who you love and who love you back because that is what valentines day really represents. I know we couldn't be together for this day Daria but I can't wait to celebrate with you this weekend I love you so much my princess! Forever & Always. Happy Valentines Day to everyone and I hope you had an astounding day just like I have"

Daria's academic awards ceremony: Nick writes: "I'm so proud to call this beautiful, intelligent, and all around amazing girl my girlfriend I couldn't ask for anything more I love you so much Daria and I can't wait to see you accomplish all of your dreams in UCF" June 6, 2016

Friends Kyle Oliver, Nick, and Guy Bogoslavsky at the Broward County Athletic Association Championships, October 2016

Preparing to swim a race with his signature blue goggles, circa fall 2017

Nick and Daria, undated photo

At the go-cart track in 2017. Front from left: Nick, Daria, Mitch, and Alex, with the pit crew in the back row

Nick emerging from the swimming stage of Utmaningen triathlon in Nora, Sweden, August 2017. Photo courtesy of Elin Pettersson

Nick with Swedish Olympian Sarah Sjöstrom, August 2017

Dworet family at an ice bar, Stockholm, Sweden, August 2017

Nick representing TS Aquatics in a Speedo Twitter contest in 2017

Nick goofing around with his newfound passion, investing, in a social media post. Notice the Lokai bracelet on his right wrist.

Nick commemorating his fifth-place finish in the 100-yard freestyle at the Florida state championships with Coach Lauren Rubenstein, November 10, 2017

Nick with his lifelong friends Ethan Searle and Leif Nilsson during the year-end holidays in 2017

Sharing his accomplishments with his family at the Florida state championships. From left, Alex, Annika, Nick, and Mitch, November 10, 2017

The last family holiday picture, 2017

Nick and his family at college signing day, Feb. 4, 2018. This is the last known family picture.

One of Nick's senior photos, which his loved ones fondly call his "James Bond" picture, 2017

CHAPTER SIX:
STUMBLE IN THE ROAD

～～～～～～～～～

"Setbacks have an upside; they fuel new dreams."

– Dara Torres

Just as Nick removed his white water polo cap, and dried himself from head to toe, his proud parents approached. The final water polo match of the season had finished, and Nick was unbeaten in swim-offs, a rare and noteworthy accomplishment. What was even more joyful was the spirit of his teammates; their morale was at an all-time high. Team standings had improved with the addition of ever-happy, ever-kind Nicholas Dworet, the star sprinter of Marjory Stoneman Douglas. Nick had been a tremendous boost to the team, leaving Coach Lauren shocked at how a single, slightly confused boy could turn the attitude of a whole team around in such a short time. But as she got to know him, she understood why; he brought an amazing spirit to the pool. The team was planning for the future with energy she had never seen before.

On the way home from the last game, Annika and Mitch decided to stop at Jerimiah's, one of Nick's favorite ice cream stores. There, they watched Nick celebrate by devouring one of his favorite combos of Italian ice and soft-serve ice cream. He asked for another, and they wisely asked him to refrain so as not to ruin dinner. Unbeknownst to his parents, Nick and his water polo friends had just been to Jerimiah's days earlier to do a taste test of the free samples. Those free samples became many more free samples; now Nick was a bit embarrassed that he had not purchased anything that day and was hoping the same people wouldn't be working. He tightened his hoodie down over his ears and forehead. Just one serving would be fine today, he agreed.

Later that month, Annika and Mitch received a preliminary copy of

Nicholas' freshman report card. His projected cumulative grade-point average for freshman year was below a 2.0. While disappointing, this news was not a complete surprise. Nick's lack of focus on his studies had been a concern from the start of the year, and his unofficial grades were not good. Nick knew he could do better but was unaware of the full extent the consequences his grades would have upon his future.

The close of freshman year was just weeks away. Nick was enjoying his new water polo friends, and also the company of the swimmers, many whom he didn't know before. His success at the sprint in water polo inspired him. Water polo had kept him in the water, along with his enthusiastic teammates. Nick did not want to let MSD down, and he knew he needed to work out. One evening, Nick told his parents that he wanted to go back to club swimming. Later, not wanting their son to see their excitement, Mitch and Annika did a private happy-dance celebration behind their bedroom doors.

Nick was headed back to the Coral Springs Swim Club. That was not, however, the plan of most of the swim team, especially Tristan Celestin. Tristan looked at the approaching 12 weeks of summer as a prime training opportunity for Nick. He was pushing hard for Nick to consider a new club program being established just south of Coral Springs by coach Andre Bailey. The team was called TS Aquatics. In his heart, Tristan felt that Nick and Coach Andre would be a good match; he just didn't know how to make it happen.

Tristan had first met Coach Andre a decade earlier when he went for his family's usual Sunday swim at Veterans Park in Lauderhill, Fla. The pool was a welcome respite from the sweltering South Florida heat for the many families who lived in the densely populated apartments that surrounded the park. Coach Andre was lifeguarding that day and noticed Tristian's natural strokes in the water. Coach Andre was new to coaching and was slowly building a swim team at this inner-city, culturally diverse aquatic center. He approached Tristian's parents and suggested that Tristian consider joining. And that was how Coach Andre found a protégé in Tristan, just 8 years old at the time, and developed him into a formidable competitive swimmer.

Coach Andre's discovery led to Tristan becoming a South Florida standout swimmer throughout his youth and high school years, holding many state and local records. As a member of the Marjory Stoneman Douglas swim team, Tristan was the one to win most races regardless of the distance or stroke. Tristan dominated at MSD, but he was ready to abdicate his position for Nicholas Dworet because he knew Nick could be better than any swimmer he had ever seen. Tristan was highly respected, but even more important than that, he respected Nick.

While Tristan's arguments for pursuing TS Aquatics were persuasive, Nick had different plans. He wanted to continue to clear his head by training again at the Coral Springs Swim Club. That club had been Nick's home forever, and he still had friends there and familiar coaches. The unknown of Coach Andre, coupled with the brand-new team, was too much, especially considering Nick was going to be spending a good part of the summer in Sweden. Although not entirely opposed to the idea of meeting Coach Andre, Nick politely told Tristan that the timing wasn't right, both in his head and in his life.

In May 2015, Nick returned to the Coral Springs Swim Club where his old pal Kyle Oliver recounted for the first time that Nick was "beatable." Oliver, proud of himself, said that this lasted for about a week because once Nick got into shape, he was back to his old self, beating most everyone in his training group. Nick also reconnected with several of his other teammates and friends, including the Chiarella sisters, Daria and Danielle. Even when he wasn't swimming, Nick began hanging out more with his swimmer friends than anyone else. Inspired by his dad and mom, Nick had become intrigued with triathlons. He decided he wanted to do the upcoming Utmaningen triathlon in Nora when he went on vacation in just a few months. Nick's circle of friends became smaller, and more sports-oriented as he began to run and cycle some, in addition to swimming.

Nick was especially excited about going to Sweden that summer because it would be the first time he would travel there by himself. The rest of his family would join him a week later. Thoughts of meeting up with his cousins, of Grandma's cooking and motorsports with Grandpa, occupied his mind as he casually ran and cycled to get in shape. Gravity-based sports such as these, while necessary, were never favored by Nick. Something in them was always missing — water. While exercising on land, the weight of his own body seemed foreign if not difficult and painful. Weightlessness and aquatic suspension seemed to make more sense to Nick. Nonetheless, he powered on with positivity, all in a state of newfound health and joy in the diversity of sports. The pressure was off of competitive swimming. Knowing that he would dominate the swimming portion of the triathlon, Nick developed a strategy for the running and cycling stages to hopefully maintain his competitiveness in the race overall. It was all new territory to him.

Nick placed second in the triathlon to a well-known seasoned triathlete; at age 15, he beat every other entrant. This made Nick something of a local celebrity, with his picture on the front page of the newspaper. Unfortunately, Nick did not make his goal to be first out of the water. He was second, but he beat that competitor overall. The day following the triathlon, Nick discovered he hadn't prepared enough for the running and cycling stages; his legs were terribly sore. During this trip, Nick took the time to research a Swedish swim team that trained near Nora. While not able to connect with the team on this trip, Nick filed away the possibility of swimming in Sweden on his next trip there. This year's vacation was just the break Nick needed, and he came home looking forward to swimming during his sophomore year at Marjory Stoneman Douglas.

While Nick was generating only positive thinking surrounding his swimming for the high school team, Coach Lauren knew of a wrench in the plan. She had been informed that Nick had been declared academically ineligible to swim in the fall of his sophomore season.

Nick and his teammates were heartbroken. His greatest challenge at this point became the classroom where he had to apply his training habits to his schoolwork. Nick became committed to improving his grades as quickly as possible. Many of his fellow swimmers offered to help, including Guy, who was in Nick's geometry and history classes. Guy offered to share his homework with Nick. Nick politely declined, owning his own problem with steadfast determination to find the solution. Nick's parents saw an abrupt change in his study habits. He would hole up in his room for hours, diligently completing his homework. Nick would also seek out ancillary assignments to prepare himself for exams as if he were preparing for swimming championships.

During this challenging time, Nick relied upon other friends who had witnessed his difficult journey during his freshman year. Kyle Oliver, ever present in Nick's life, was attending another high school. Known by his last name far more often than his first, Oliver loved to be with Nick, outside of the pool. A self-proclaimed brainiac, Oliver had a positive influence on Nick. In addition, Oliver was always up for fun while retaining an impressive moral compass. Oliver was strappingly tall, standing well over 6 feet 2 inches and weighing nearly 200 pounds. He was a backstroker, whose reach and strong shoulders showed promise for years in club swimming. However, his commitment was to the books not the water. One of his most favorite things to do with Nick was eat and observe Nick's legendary appetite. For Oliver, it was another form of spectator sport.

One time that fall, the two went to Wayback Burger for Nick to participate in the annual Triple Triple Challenge. Each year, the restaurant chain holds a nationwide contest to see who can consume the iconic nine-patty burger, complete with nine slices of American cheese and topped with lettuce and tomato. The fastest competitor would be awarded $3,300.

Nick, applying his sprinter skills, knew that the prize dollars were within reach. In fact, in his mind, he had already spent the prize money when he walked up to the counter. He ordered the near $20 burger and excitement mounted. Oliver stood by and watched someone else's Triple Triple come out of the kitchen and wondered how Nick was going to eat such a thing so fast.

Finally, Nick's number was called — and there it was. A piping-hot, Triple Triple, oozing with mustard, mayonnaise, ketchup, and cheese. When Nick took the first bite, his burger was too hot to eat. Nick decided to douse the behemoth meal with water. The bun disintegrated,

the condiments and cheese followed, and the tower began to fall. All
the while, Nick was attempting to hurriedly eat the 5,100-calorie burger.
In slow motion, the nine cheeseburgers tumbled in an assorted mess
all over the table. The mess transferred to Nick's hands and face. Nick's
time ended up being several minutes. They later learned the winner was a
young woman (purportedly a "skinny" girl, according to Oliver) who ate
the sandwich in 48 seconds. Nick swore revenge and said his next eating
contest would be at an ice cream parlor across the street; he intended to
enter the following week. Oliver was thankful that the business closed
before Nick could go there. Oliver considered competitive eating to be
painful to watch.

Around this time, Nick began to run into senior Daria Chiarella more
frequently at club swim practice. In the past, despite their two-year age
difference, they had often trained in the same group. They had enjoyed a
nice friendship over the years.

Daria began competing in swimming as a freshman in high school.
Realizing that her best opportunity to develop in the sport was through
club swimming, she joined the Coral Springs Swim Club. There, she
became a champion in her own right, receiving the girls' senior 2A award
in 2015. Daria and Nick attended different high schools. College-bound
Daria had outstanding grades and her course load included plenty of
Advanced Placement classes. Daria was a beautiful, petite, long-haired
brunette, who lent an empathetic ear to most anyone but especially Nick.
She listened intently to his dilemma regarding grades and swimming but
offered no advice; she just listened. Daria was at times shy and reserved
but had the poise and maturity of someone much older.

The larger group of their swimmer friends seemed to melt away as
Daria and Nick began to hang out together, just the two of them. Nick
posted a puzzling comment on social media: "Nothing else to do locked
up in my room with some thoughts of u."

The Overcheerer

Determined to make his way back to the MSD swim team, Nick largely kept his ineligibility quiet. However, on meet days he was seen sitting in the stands cheering. He was forlorn that he couldn't compete but managed to keep most of those feelings inside by cheering so often and loudly he was labeled the "overcheerer." When his teammates looked up at him, they thought he looked only a little bit sad; they were truly the sad ones. In fact, Nick was mad, but only at himself. As the season progressed, he processed those feelings into a positive yearning. A fire grew in his belly to return to compete for his school. People described his determination to right his wrong at the time as remarkable. More than anything, Nick wanted to swim for his high school.

Nick successfully kept his ineligibility from his club teammates, except Daria. Worried about Coach Chris' reaction that he wasn't swimming at high school, Nick also skipped club workouts on the days of high school swim meets. Even though he didn't want to skip practice, Nick's desire to swim was less than his concern about his coach's wrath should he learn that Nick was academically ineligible. So, Nick kept his situation quiet and kept competing in local club competitions.

In November 2015, Nick swam in the winter championships. He performed well overall at this meet. For the first time in competition, he broke the five-minute barrier in the 500-yard free, bettering his personal best time by almost five seconds; he placed fifth. Nick improved his times in all his events as well. Just a month later, Nick received his report card. His grades had improved to a passing level, which meant he would be eligible to play water polo in the spring. Nick was relieved, but the question still remained: Had he fully recovered from his stumble?

On to the National Training Group

Nick discovered that his swimming performance at the winter championships had made him eligible to move up to the national training group at the Coral Springs Swim Club, a dream come true. However, Nick was making this move solo; gone were the other three from his Circle of Four. He also would not be training anywhere nearby Daria. Since ringing in the new year, their friendship was growing deeper. It was exciting and nerve-wracking all at once. This move created additional pressure, pressure to commit and pressure to perform. Nick discovered his eligibility for the national team when the coach had called to see why he was not coming to two-a-day practices. The swimmer practices before school and after for a combined three to five hours each day. It is a grueling existence, but it unequivocally works to develop champions. Swimming is a sport of repetition and of conditioning, and the athlete must do both to succeed. Nick knew this, but he had other mounting distractions that were surrounding his heart.

Nick went to swim practice once per day for now, as the water polo season was set to begin soon. He was anticipating being the sprinter again, and he knew that water polo would be more fun with less pressure. Daria was supportive of Nick's progress with his grades and his upbeat attitude toward competing in the pool at whatever sport that may be.

While Nick tried to balance his club swimming workouts with water polo, it was difficult. The national group was extremely serious; swimmers there were not receptive to the silly jokes Nick had been used to telling during warmups. Out of design, the fun was now gone; the national training group was all business. There wasn't much talking; English wasn't necessary; the clock was a universal communicator. Nick attempted to reestablish the language of swimming with his lane mates. It just wasn't the same, and Nick noticed that the one thing these swimmers had in common was a predatorlike competitiveness promoted by Coach Bruno.

Every stroke, every breath, and every lap mattered like life and death. There was no letting up. There was no friendliness; these swimmers would swim over you, not around you. In the locker room there was silence and no eye contact. There was no friendly chitchat. Everyone was in their own little world and couldn't see past their own tired bodies.

After a while, this style of training became more familiar. Nick knew what to expect, yet he didn't know what to enjoy. His competition times began to show this ambivalence, Nick started to question whether he wanted it, whatever "it" was, because he had yet to have a conversation with his coach about his goals.

Meanwhile, during one important water polo game, Nick had won the sprint and was able to get into scoring position. The goalie successfully defended Nick's attempt at scoring from the wing position. When looking at the goal, the wing is the farthest angle to the left or right, the sneakiest and most difficult position from which to score. Nick's failure wasn't entirely the reason his team lost the game, but he did not like to lose. Nick felt responsible as a leader of sorts. The sprinter is usually the most revered member of the water polo team, and Nick's devotion to the team made the loss hard to swallow; he thought he had cost MSD the game. The ride home in the team van seemed long and pensive. Nick customarily rode in the front passenger seat of the van, next to Coach Lauren. She looked over at Nick and noticed him twisting a bracelet on his wrist. It was the first time she had seen this bracelet. She asked him what he was doing and he explained that it was a Lokai bracelet that contained two sacred beads. Nick was concentrating on the beads. He explained that the white bead contains water from Mount Everest, representing the high points in life, and the black bead contains a speck of mud from the Dead Sea, signifying the difficult moments. The elements are designed to guide people through life with balance; to stay humble through those highs and hopeful through the lows. At this very moment, Nick was feeling low, and he needed the black bead to help him through the loss of the game. Nick revealed that his friend Daria had given it to him, and that she also had a matching one. From then on, Nick rarely removed his Lokai bracelet.

A Natural Leader

Geoff Hayman, by now the graduating senior captain of the water polo team, said Nick had a lot to teach him. Geoff learned from watching Nick: how he took criticism and how he dealt with defeats. For example, the day after the heartbreaking loss, Nick asked Geoff to go to the pool and repeat the play that had failed. Geoff got into the pool and assumed the position of goalie. They then practiced the play Nick had missed, repeatedly, so that he could get past the defender and score. Nick never wanted to fail at that play again. Nick didn't complain, he didn't make excuses; he worked harder and harder trying to improve. Nick needed to perfect that play. The word "blame" was not in his vocabulary.

Geoff felt Nick was the swimmer who must replace him as captain for MSD water sports. Nick had all the ingredients to become a captain of water polo, swimming, or both, and Geoff needed to have a conversation with Coach Lauren soon, so he could secure his legacy and leave the teams in good hands. Balancing competitive club swimming with water polo was tricky. Nick made it to club practice sporadically, in between water polo matches. All the while, he was also working on his grades, which were steadily improving. Nick also competed in swim meets throughout South Florida with frustrating results. Over the second half of his sophomore year, many of Nick's times became a bit slower and slower. The frustrating turning point came in March 2016, where Nick had one of the most disappointing meets of his life at the Southern Zone South Sectional Championships. By the middle of May, he swam his last meet for the Coral Springs Swim Club. With indecision, he decided to take a break from club swimming.

However, Nick's indecision about the pool was offset by an important decision on land. Over the past several months, Nick had found his friendship with Daria to be the light of his life. There wasn't a secret between them, nor a conscious or subconscious thought unexplored. They knew every crevice of each other's soul; their friendship was tugging hard at Nick's heartstrings. Nick wanted more, and a message he posted on social media revealed his inner thoughts:

"Inner piece [sic] and happiness. I'm always tryna' find it. And I kinda got the feeling that a woman is behind it."

Just one month later, he and Daria officially became boyfriend and girlfriend. As the passionate martial artist Bruce Lee once said, "Their love was born out of a friendship which caught on fire. In the beginning it was a flame, very pretty, often hot and fierce, but sustained through bright light and flickering." It continued that way forever.

Nick soon found himself immersed in Daria's senior year. Because he was only a sophomore, Nick was on unfamiliar ground. Daria was still concentrating on her studies, trying to increase her GPA by an additional one-tenth of a point. She already was slated to graduate in the top 10% of her class, and her college entry was secured. But she was a serious, determined student. Her habits had rubbed off on Nick. He continued to study with structure and zeal, but sometimes the playful, carefree Nick would come out while he was waiting for Daria at her mother's house. Daria's mom was a fantastic cook, and she would frequently have a meal or large snack prepared. As Nick ate, Daria studied, and then they both went out to eat. This worked well for a champion eater.

Nick and Daria had casually discussed her upcoming prom, but a "promposal" was the current standard. Nick was to formally ask Daria with a public presentation of sorts. For over two years, Nick had maintained his fascination with apparel from the Supreme label. Nick created a poster with many pictures of him and Daria, and a partially handwritten statement that read: "Prom will be Supreme with you." The word Supreme was represented by a logo sticker. Of course, her answer was a resounding yes.

Nick found preparing for the prom exciting. He purchased his first suit in a charcoal gray. He carefully chose a blue tie to match Daria's dress; light blue was his favorite color. Daria's dress was a showstopper. Together, the couple was stunning. Nick learned what a corsage was, and a boutonniere, ordering both from a local florist. Final preparations for the evening were completed at Daria's house where a hairdresser and makeup artist tried to calm Daria, who was unaccustomed to such a fuss. She emerged, beautiful as ever, and greeted by parents and her excited date. Off they went in a limousine with some of their friends for an evening of a lifetime.

Not long after prom, Daria graduated with honors from J.P. Taravella High School in Coral Springs. Daria had little time to spare between high school and college. Her first term at the University of Central Florida was to begin in July, so she and Nick made the best of their last eight weeks together. A highlight was a Dworet family trip to Orlando, which coincided with Daria's move. In July 2015, Daria started college, and she and Nick began their long-distance relationship. Nick said: "Distance isn't an issue cause in the end, I have you. I love you babe."

CHAPTER SEVEN:
BUTTERFLY

"Have faith in yourself; faith in the infinite... Faith is the eternal elixir. It gives life, power and action to the impulse of thought."

– Napoleon Hill, American self-help author

It was the fall of 2016. Nick was academically eligible. He knew his high school teammates were counting on him. He constantly dreamed about swimming but upon waking, there was always an unresolved ending. Nick was confused, and he actively sought to understand his feelings.

While some teenagers may consider quitting under such pressure, and while Nick had in the past taken breaks from swimming, he now chose to conquer his ambivalence with excitement. Nick realized that the swimmer within him needed to swim. He was in an improved space with his family, his friends, his teammates, and with his life. More than ever before, Nick was looking forward for school to begin.

On the first day of Nick's junior year, he took in the sights of his now familiar high school that seemed so large and overwhelming just two years ago. He remembered his feelings about swimming and water polo, and how he had dealt with his malaise and questions of commitment. He recalled the agony of not being able to swim during the past year, and excitement about having a blank slate. As his body had grown up, so had his mind. He had a healthy perspective about swimming for MSD, and knew it was time to get to work. However, he was still ambivalent about club swimming.

Tristan Celestin returned to Nick with the same proposition of a year ago, to consider swimming for Coach Andre Bailey at TS Aquatics. Tristan was the perfect choice to corral Nick back into club swimming. Tristan, now a senior, was a charismatic leader and the de facto king of swimming at MSD. Tristan had been a legendary star swimmer from the moment he set foot at high school, but set his ego aside to guide Nick, knowing that his potential in the pool exceeded that of any swimmer he had ever seen. Tristan knew that Nick soon would be beating him and he was ready to abdicate his throne.

At the same time, Tristan tried to make headway with Nick, he sent a text message to Coach Andre:

Tristan: "Remember that guy I told you about? I think he's finally ready."

Andre replied: "You know where I'm at. Always willing to talk."

Tristan to Andre: "He's special. He needs help."

Andre to Tristan: "Everyone is special. Everyone needs help. He just needs to come. I don't treat anyone as special, you know that."

Andre to Tristan again: "He has to follow the program. NO EXCEPTIONS. LMK when he's coming."

Tristan to Andre: "His name is Nicholas Dworet."

Shortly after this exchange, a visit was set up for Nick to watch a swim workout in process and to meet Coach Andre. Annika appeared on the scene first, like she was taking a dog to the vet, dragging an apprehensive Nick behind her. Nick was coaxed onto the pool deck, and Annika and a distracted Coach Andre had a long conversation. The evening was balmy, and insects buzzed around the well-lit picnic table adjacent to the pool. Nick hardly spoke as he tried to "chase the ambivalence."

According to Coach Andre, he made it clear that TS (Total Swimmer) Aquatics was an up-and-coming club program and he didn't have the time or energy to make exceptions. He didn't want to coddle a talented boy with no ambition. To Coach Andre, Nick looked like a disheveled, long-haired, 150-pound rebel. Coach Andre told him, "You're either in or you're out."

Nick eventually tried a workout. Coach Andre believed that a swimmer's work in the pool was only half or less of what was important; who you were as a person, and the work performed outside of the pool mattered at least equally. As a result, Coach Andre trained his wards in schoolwork, personal growth, and integrity; there were very few details about his swimmers' lives that went unnoticed by this dedicated coach. Their struggles were his struggles, both in and out of the pool.

Coach Andre seemed like a father with the capacity for an endless number of children. He first began competing in his native Jamaica at a very young age. He favored breaststroke and became accomplished in his home country before his family immigrated to South Florida when he was 12. Under the tutelage of Coach Lohberg, Coach Andre joined the Coral Springs Swim Club in the 1990s, and he became a formidable breaststroker throughout his teenage years. He competed in the Florida State championships three out of four years of high school, a significant accomplishment. Uncomfortable talking about himself, Coach Andre downplays his swimming record, "Great swimmers do not always make great coaches, and I was not a great swimmer." When asked if he ever considered returning to compete for the Jamaican National Team, Coach Andre said, "It was a remote possibility, but one that I never really considered or dreamed of then; the international fluidity of the South Florida swimming community was not well established, making such a venture difficult, if not impossible."

Becoming a Total Swimmer

Nick began to show up to practice with regularity. After showing the requisite commitment, he was paired with Diego, a sprinter who was faster than Nick with an impeccable work ethic. Diego was the perfect embodiment of Coach Andre's Total Swimmer program and was capable of pushing Nick and demonstrating the attitude and aptitude to succeed there. It was at this time that Nick began regularly training with weights. He also radically changed his diet. As a result, his body began to change. Nick became leaner, his shoulders grew wider, and his leg, arm, and back muscles became more defined. The transformation was swift and dramatic. One day, Nick's dad looked at him and said to himself, "Who is this boy? When did this happen?"

Nick had little time to waste at TS. Club training was a supplement for his competition at high school, and competition was beginning soon. A lot was riding on this season for Nick, and for others. One day, Coach Lauren introduced Nick to Kenan Kocoglu, a 14-year-old freshman in need of some direction and assistance with joining TS Aquatics. Yet, consistent with Nick's nature, even though he had no time to spare, he made Kenan feel like he had all the time in the world for him.

Kenan, who was born in Germany, was the oldest of three children. He began competing in swimming late. In fact, it was hardly a year before entering Marjory Stoneman Douglas. He was a skinny, tall, shy boy, two years younger than Nick. Kenan showed much promise in the sport but had a lot of catching up to do. Each day after school, Kenan needed a ride from Douglas to the TS club practice; Nick cheerfully offered to be Kenan's chauffeur. The boys had roughly 20 minutes from the last-period bell to get to the pool. Strangers at first, the two boys developed a strong friendship which stretched way beyond swimming. Kenan called Nick his "older brother from another mother."

Nick didn't like to be late to practice, but Kenan was always running late because his last class was a long distance across the sprawling campus to where Nick parked his car. Further, MSD was easily a 20-minute drive to the TS pool, even on the lightest of traffic days. Kenan would hustle to meet Nick, and then Nick would drive his beloved silver Volvo faster than the speed limit with the windows down and rap music playing loudly. If the boys were late, Coach Andre made them each do 25 push-ups. If one of the boys gave the coach lip he threatened to "add a zero to the end of it," making it 250 push-ups.

Upon joining TS Aquatics, Kenan got stuck in Lane 5, the slow lane.

Hard on himself, he was embarrassed to see his friends swimming four lanes over in Lane 1. Kenan enjoyed doing strength and conditioning, aka dryland, with Nick and the other swimmers. Sometimes they would run distances outside and sprints after, pushing each other competitively. It was in these moments, with his head out of the water, that Kenan watched and learned the most from Nick about inner dialogue and how to deal with poor performance. Taken to criticizing himself, Kenan watched Nick lose these foot races. Rather than belittle himself, Nick just talked about what he did wrong, noting "I'll get them next time." Nick had a calmness when he won and never indulged in displays of throwing things or other physical displays of anger when he lost. Kenan said, "I learned fast that my habit of making excuses was not a part of how Nick viewed himself. He made no excuses, he only identified ways to perform better in the future. That will stick with me forever."

The pressure upon 14-year-old Kenan to move out of the slow lane, produced the fastest trajectory of improvement Coach Andre had ever seen. Over time, Kenan also transformed from an unsure, shy, self-critical boy to a young man, who was a confident team leader. Coach Andre also began to notice the younger kids at practice waiting for the arrival of Nick's car. Nick and Kenan usually came screeching into the parking lot with less than 5 minutes to spare before practice was to begin, and quickly parked. The kids calmed down and there was a sense of order and completeness. The younger children were shy and in awe, the middle lane (or slightly older children) felt like the practice was going to be a good one, and Nick's peers over in Lanes 1 and 2 were ready to "kick ass." It was time to go all-out. Nick's coaches were ready to dish it out and see what the end result would be. As Nick and his lane mates jumped into the pool, adrenaline was on the rise. There was a freedom like no other when Nick's body became enveloped by the water. Soon Kenan would move up through the lanes to train closer to Nick.

Another swimmer at TS was quietly observing his new teammate. His name was Carlos Vasquez. Carlos attended St. Thomas Aquinas High School, an acclaimed Catholic high school known for both academics and athletics. A serious student and a serious swimmer, Carlos had witnessed a steady stream of Coral Springs Swim Club members venturing south to test the waters with this upstart team. The work ethic of the Coral Springs swimmers seemed different, more relaxed. The TS swimmers called them "slackers." Many didn't go all-out or try their hardest which was difficult to understand for the TS swimmers. Most didn't last at TS. Carlos said, "I thought Nick was one of those slackers." He glanced at Nick and wondered how long he would last. Was he made of the same lackadaisical work ethic as the others? Would he be gone in a week? Carlos quickly learned that Nick was different. His drive showed up loud and clear. Nick soon shared their language of swimming over in Lane 1.

Nick was happy, and for the first time both his mind and body were immersed in a positive and fulfilling swim program. He focused closely on his attendance at practice, his nutrition, and excluded with a vengeance any outside influences that could detract from swimming. Nick also began to exhibit leadership skills among his TS teammates, including helping younger swimmers with their strokes and consoling upset swimmers after a disappointing race.

Coach Andre was taking note. The coach loved exploring the realm of potential in each and every swimmer, and as his relationship with Nick evolved, Coach Andre found a new meaning for the word "potential." Coach Andre had never seen potential like Nick's — boundless, slightly intimidating, and very exciting. Most importantly, Nick seemed unaware of his potential. Coach Andre described his coaching style as one of consistency: "The swimmer comes first, and the coach has to be consistent day in and day out, regardless of what is happening outside of the pool in his or her own life. In turn, the swimmers will respond and trust the program." This is exactly what happened to Nick. For the first time, he had a coach who was consistent, a "third parent" Nick could trust. Coach Andre also adhered to principles of honesty. He felt it incorrect to foster false dreams in a swimmer whom he knew would never reach a certain level, such as the Olympics. However, Coach Andre also believed that potential is not a tangible thing, and that you never know how far a swimmer is going to go. Being able to adjust expectations is key to maintaining a healthy coaching relationship.

Coach Andre called Nick, Carlos, Diego, and a few other young swimmers the "OGs," short for "Original Gangsters," which in slang terms is defined as praise for someone considered excellent, but which holds sentimental value for the coach. These were his special young men, with a private group nickname, who had unwavering faith in Coach Andre and vice versa. This faith transcended the pool into every facet of these young men's lives. On a visceral level, Nick enjoyed being one of Coach Andre's "OGs" and a treasured member of TS Aquatics. Tristan's instincts were right. He had successfully orchestrated Nick into finding a new loving home for club swimming. In Coach Andre, Nick had found the third parent he had been seeking for most of his life.

Upon closer examination, Coach Andre noticed that if Nick made some corrections to his strokes, it could improve his times. Over years of repetitive training, sometimes swimmers can improve minute flaws, and sometimes they cannot; muscle memory is a strong animal. Coach Andre related that Nick was one of the receptive swimmers. He was "thirsty for instruction." For example, Nick needed to change the entry of his hands in freestyle and butterfly to a sharper angle (they were flat and needed to be more cupped and angled downward), which allowed for a better catch. The results of this change were instant and magical. Both coach and swimmer were elated.

Other changes, such as the rhythm of Nick's kick, were more frustrating, and took months to change. In sprinting, the kick is fast while in distance races it is slow and rhythmic. If a swimmer cannot slow his kick down in a distance race, he will consume oxygen unnecessarily which will impact his performance. Coach Andre and Nick worked on this over and over, but results were hard to measure. Even still, this sort of collaborative, rote instruction was fuel for Nick; he had never had it before. Swimming is a sport of perfection, and any champion will tell you they were always chasing it, including Nick.

Coach Andre described Nick as unique, "One moment you could be having a perfect adult conversation with him, and the next moment you would look over and he's being a kid with his teammates." There were times when Coach Andre was running a few minutes late, and he asked Nick to get his teammates moving toward starting practice. Nick, now regularly called "Swim Daddy" by his younger teammates, would direct the swimmers to suit up, gather their gear, assemble by their practice lanes, and start loosening their shoulders and stretching their legs. In these moments, Coach Andre could trust Nick and only Nick with this pre-workout leadership.

Swimming needs to be fun, and Nick had moments where he was a teenager to the core. Coach Andre required the older swimmers to be model citizens for the youngsters. Cussing and inappropriate language was not tolerated anywhere associated with the team. Instead, proper methods for dealing with anger and disappointment were monitored among the swimmers and coaches.

One day, however, Nick and the OGs changed the lyrics to a popular rap song and began singing it on deck during practice. The new lyrics were raunchy and inappropriate. Coach Andre tried, without success, to shield the youngsters swimming a few lanes over. Still, the boys continued to sing, and when they didn't stop, they were threatened with push-ups, and then more push-ups, and then finally expulsion from practice. They stopped singing only when the push-up count reached an excess of 500. Coach Andre addressed them as "gentlemen," as each performed their push-ups. Nick cracked yet another joke and the laughter and giggling that permeated the group caused Andre to start the exercise over again. There were several starts and stops. By the end, the entire group had done an inhumane number of push-ups; they only swam for 15 minutes out of a two-hour practice.

The next morning, Nick woke up with the sorest arms and shoulders he had ever experienced. A long hot shower followed by self-massage didn't help. Finally, as he jumped into the pool later that day and slowly rotated one arm after another, his body warmed up. Nick glanced at his Lokai bracelet on his left hand and didn't know whether he needed the white bead or the black bead at this very moment, but he was reminded of the wisdom the bracelet represented. His blood flowed through his push-up-punished muscles and slowly carried away the lactic acid that was making him so sore. By the end of the workout, Nick was swimming with power again, and the OGs were at it, pushing each other all-out; later they would agree the push-ups had a purpose.

Early in the school year, Nick had a tragedy to deal with. On Sept. 16, 2016, Chris Jackson, Nick's coach from Coral Springs, died unexpectedly at the age at 39. Chris was the first coach to believe in Nick, and Nick reflected upon this as he mourned the loss. This erased all doubt from Nick's mind that he had closed his final chapter on the Coral Springs Swim Club.

By October, both club and high school competitions were under way. Nick was competing for Marjory Stoneman Douglas with stellar results. The dual meets continued with ease, and Nick was looking forward to swimming with Tristan, Guy, and his other teammates, and hopefully at the state championships. Tristan had announced this was the sunset of his competitive swimming career; he was quitting after graduation.

Nick's first club competition as a TS swimmer was on Oct.14. He swam four events and had a good meet. In the 50-yard free, Nick's specialty, he was able to out-touch his training partner Diego, who finished two places and .12 seconds behind him. The boys got out of the pool and congratulated each other with the typical handshake and with arms over shoulders as they headed to cool down. Coach Andre met them and said, "Good job, gentlemen." As a reward for returning to competition with enthusiasm, Annika and Mitch encouraged Nick to purchase a long-sleeve T-shirt from this swim meet in his favorite light blue color. It said, "I'm so good your mom even cheers for me." This was an ironic selection given that Nick was a consummate humble swimmer, and truly didn't understand just how good he was.

A New Friend and a New Passion

Meanwhile, outside of the pool, Carlos and Nick were becoming closer friends. They had developed several post-practice routines. One was to find bubble tea. Bubble tea, also known as boba on the West Coast, is an odd beverage with an acquired taste, but satisfying for any starving swimmer. Invented in Taiwan during the 1980s, the tea is shaken with ice to create bubbles. A foamy layer emerges and chewy tapioca balls, called "boba" or "pearls," are added which often sink to the bottom. The pearls are large and jelly-like and come in many flavors, so as the liquid is consumed the pearls are left to eat like Jell-O.

As their friendship grew, the new friends decided to detour after practice. The irony is that this was only possible on a school night because Carlos was alone at home, a fact that Nick did not yet know. Nor did Nick know that his friendship, and bubble tea, were becoming a foundation which was normalizing Carlos' life. In February of 2017, the boys' junior year, Carlos' younger sister required an organ transplant and later experienced complications. His parents and his sister temporarily relocated to New York for her treatment which lasted until December, leaving Carlos alone for long periods of time in the family's large house. He got himself to school, and then swimming at TS Aquatics after school. Nick seemed to understand Carlos' loneliness and fear without asking. Nick helped Carlos get through life during this frightening period, a fact that Nick may not have ever known. Carlos also introduced Nick to his other newfound passion, investing.

At St. Thomas Aquinas High School, Carlos had taken a popular economics class from an accomplished educator named Robert Williams. Williams had inspired Carlos and others to take on economics as a life pursuit. Williams' success as a teacher was reflected in the success of his students; their AP test scores were consistently among the highest in the nation. Carlos described Williams as creating an eye-opening experience which he will never forget.

While sipping bubble tea one day, and even though he was physically exhausted from practice, a normally calm and collected Carlos could not contain his excitement. He began to share his experience with Nick. Carlos had just finished reading "Rich Dad, Poor Dad" by Robert Kiyosaki and Sharon Lechter. He lent the book to Nick. Careful not to spill the sticky tea on its pages, Nick was intrigued and eager to read it. Nick's parents said it was one of the few books Nick ever read outside of school. He read it with vigor.

Nick was officially initiated into the world of financial literacy. After that, Nick and Carlos developed their own language involving business terminology, sayings, and idioms. Their chatter was unstoppable. "You can work for the man 9-5 or you can be the man," became their mantra. They shared social media posts regarding financial planning and dreamed of becoming rich. Nick also began to proselytize to his friends and family. Coach Lauren fondly recalled driving to swim meets in the MSD van, with Nick sitting shotgun, discussing business theory with seemingly the same passion he had for swimming.

Carlos cherished these trips for bubble tea, just him and Nick, and economics. Soon, other swimmers began to catch on and came along after practice, mostly for the tea. While it wasn't as much fun since only Carlos and Nick shared a passion for business talk, a special bond had been formed, bringing a smile to the shy yet soulful Carlos.

One afternoon, Nick strolled into a used bookstore in Coral Springs and bought the legendary book, "Think and Grow Rich," by Napoleon Hill. It would be a book that resonated strongly with Nick. In fact, he never put it down.

CHAPTER EIGHT:
BACKSTROKE

"Insanity is doing the same thing over and over and expecting different results."

– author Rita Mae Brown

Swimmers have long been determined to prove this axiom wrong. Any coach will maintain that the only way to improve in the sport is to engage in repetitious training; it develops strength, speed, and perfection. After working out hard each weekday, swimmers hope to see their results in the form of personal-record times (PRs) at the weekend swim meets. For Nick and others like him, the hours spent working out often led to steady improvement, even if such improvement was only in one one-hundredths of a second. The axiom was proven wrong by swimmers who demonstrated that different results can be attained by doing the same thing over and over, even if those results were infinitesimal.

As swimmers become more mature, they realize the repetition and the physical struggle anticipated in each workout never becomes any easier to endure. Like swimmers everywhere, the athletes at TS Aquatics rustled the energy from their exhausted and sore bodies each day, sometimes twice a day, to again suffer the monotony of swimming back and forth in the pool, like a metronome on a piano. Nick bought into it, swimming full force despite fatigue, investing 100% of his mind and body into his sport. Nick viewed his workouts as an opportunity to visit with his soul and to converse with his private self about his exciting future. Sometimes he imagined the five Olympic rings, embedded in his mind, as he made turn after turn, and start after start in the pool. He memorized the colors of the rings (from left to right: blue, yellow, black, green, and red), and thought it inspiring that each one represented a continent. When joined together, the rings signify world unity. Nick dreamed of when he could be a part of the Olympics; where he would likely swim for a country other than America, and experience first-hand the broader meaning of the Olympic Games. By design, Nick was constantly reminded of his Olympic ambitions because he had changed his phone screensaver to the logo of the Tokyo 2020 Olympics.

These hours of contemplation led Nick to become familiar with his awesome, positive drive. Nick embraced this drive; it fueled him. It also enabled him to focus upon his academics. Nick was becoming a man. One day while in math class, Nick had finished solving the assigned problems early. In the space remaining next to his answers, he doodled "49.99" on every line on the page. At the very top, he drew the Olympic rings, and examples of his signature could be seen randomly scribbled. The time "49.99" was his best guess of the time he needed in the 100-meter free to enter the highest level of competition in Sweden or the United States. Also, he may have been practicing his autograph at the top of the page, next to the Olympic rings; with ambitions like Nick's, one can't practice their autograph enough.

Nick also used his time in the water to dream about love. He always spoke to Daria just before entering the pool, and later as he dried off after practice. Daria was on his mind constantly, and the pleasure he had thinking of her spilled over into his performance. In practice, as he pushed off from the wall, his teammates found him hard to catch up to most of the time. They appreciated Nick's refined swimming language, but they could not always replicate it; strong arms turning over faster than everyone else, toned and streamlined legs churning with a big kick, and an explosive breakout after his flip turn. The acceleration from pushing off the wall was a skill that Coach Andre had concentrated on with Nick. Once mastered, a breakout is seen as one of the main advantages for competitive swimmers. It takes strength and cardiac capacity to master them. Nick had both. Now, it took all the energy and speed that Carlos, Diego, Kenan, and others had to keep up with Nick.

As Nick's first local meet as a TS swimmer was under his belt, Nick became more intense. Each and every workout mattered. Nick arrived early to practice and left late. Even so, he always had time for the younger swimmers who had questions or just wanted some of his time; they were drawn to him like a magnet. Now everyone, including the pool staff, called him "Swim Daddy." Nick's commitment to the younger swimmers fortified him as a legend.

Workouts at TS Aquatics have been called many names: inhumane, brutal, punishing, torture, and so forth. However, all serious swimmers in the throes of midseason training would say the same of their training; in other words, punishing workouts were not unique to TS. As champion swimmer Tera Bradham once said, "Swimmer: It's a word that encompasses a brutality known only by those to whom it pertains." Champion swimmers know that this kind of training works. Swimming, like many sports, has a sense of fairness. Training brings results. The clock doesn't argue.

Before touching the water, Nick, Kenan, Diego, Carlos, and many of their teammates lifted weights for upwards of an hour, pushing their muscles to a high level of fatigue. Through self-massage and drinking water mixed with electrolyte powder, they attempted a quick fix for their muscles before their bodies got punished again in the pool.

The heating effect of the Florida sun necessitates that most pools have a chiller, which lowers the water temperature to make training more comfortable. Without a chiller, the pool would be too warm for a swim team to practice. For Nick and his friends, swimming in the pool after weights was a welcome respite. When Nick dove into the pool, he felt a glorious sensation of cool water running over his weightless, buoyant body. Coming up for his first breath, he began turning and reaching out and stretching his sore biceps and lat (latissimus dorsi) muscles through the water. During his first few strokes, he noticed his ever-present Lokai bracelet on his left wrist to guide him through practice. Nick's quads, hamstrings and glutes thanked him with the first gentle kicks. Slowly, his body seemed less sore, and he began to cool down from the heat and tightness acquired from his workout with weights. The sweat, that had previously been pouring off his red face, was gone.

Coach Andre only gave Lane 1 — the fastest OG boys — a short but necessary warmup before pushing them to their limits again in the water. The brutality was about to begin and Nick knew it as he turned his Lokai bracelet to find the white bead. This bead reminded Nick that if he were on top he needed to be humble, and now Nick was almost always on top, a star in practice and elsewhere in his life.

Coach Andre said practices "usually follow a routine because that way the kids know what is coming and are mentally prepared." After warmup, the swimmers would perform drills which isolated parts of their strokes promoting improvement in technique. As the drills ended, the swimmers knew that the real work lay ahead. Next was the highly anticipated main set which served as the focus for the day. Every swimmer deals with the anticipation of the main set differently; Nick was usually excited. Research has shown that the way athletes talk to themselves about pain has a strong mind-body connection, directly impacting how much pain they actually feel. Thus, if Nick were to tell himself it was going to hurt, it would hurt even more. However, Nick's attitude of excitement was healthy, and it likely diminished his perception of pain. Again, Nick became an example for the rest of the team.

One of Coach Andre's favorite main sets was a conditioning workout. This was a series of 200-meter repeats in which the lane mates would begin at a fast pace of less than 3 minutes per 200 and endure increasingly faster intervals until they reached 2:25 for the 20th repeat. This meant that by the end of swimming 4,000 meters (over 2 miles), the boys were swimming at a brisk pace. Their red faces had returned, now appearing purple. They were sweating profusely but couldn't see or feel it; their sweat was pouring off into the pool. In hopes of cooling their bodies, many used their exhausted shoulders to push up out of the pool, just to feel any breeze. Sometimes, one would discretely vomit in the corner; especially if he were out of shape. The gigantic water bottles at the edge of the pool, which at the beginning of practice looked impossibly large to empty, would be thoroughly drained by the end. Sometimes a gust of wind would blow the empty water bottles across the pool deck.

Like his fellow lane mates, Nick pondered how he was going to make it through the challenging set. Careful not to verbalize his thoughts, Nick put his head down and used his positivity as fuel to grind through the set. As he got toward the end and saw that he was going to complete it, he became exhilarated beyond belief. Sensing Nick's excitement, Coach Andre peered down from the deck, shouting, "Come on, you can do it!" These words of encouragement meant the world to Nick.

In Nick's mind, tomorrow, and all of the following days, he knew he was going to be facing hours of physical and mental torture. But unlike the past, at this place in his life, this challenge motivated Nick. Every day, Nick was going to rouse his incredibly sore body out of bed to get to the pool. In fact, the thought of not swimming did not enter his consciousness. Nick needed to swim in order to live.

Swimming Was Life and Life Was Swimming

At the end of hard sets, Nick saw glimmers of smiles among Carlos, Diego, and others, and he knew through their physical language that each of them felt the same — a wonderful sense of accomplishment and success. Nick also saw improvement in his friends. With more frequency, Nick caught a smile on Coach Andre's face, behind the ever-present mirrored sunglasses. Even if a word wasn't spoken, Nick knew his coach was proud of the effort put into completing these brutal sets and that he, too, was along for the ride. Coach Andre believed in his boys. Nick knew Coach Andre's commitment ran deep and that he would never leave or disappear from his life.

As he became deeply immersed in the TS program, Nick began to earn more rest between intervals, a subtle sign that he was becoming faster. This was, unfortunately, not always his pal Kenan's experience. While he no longer swam behind the slower swimmers in Lane 4, and was improving at lightning speed, Kenan still wanted more than anything to join his friend Nick in Lane 1. Kenan would bargain with Coach Andre to swim the hardest main set of the workout in Lane 1. In the beginning, his lane mates, including Nick, would lap Kenan. When this happened, Coach Andre had no choice but to move Kenan to Lane 2, a slower lane. Many would be humiliated by this, but Kenan was angry and inspired to get back to Lane 1 instead. Nick would talk Kenan up on their ride back home after practice, and soon, after working excruciatingly hard, Kenan was able to keep up with the pace of Lane 1. The first time Kenan made the intervals, and stopped at the wall, each lane mate cheered along with Coach Andre. While not an original gangster, Kenan had become one of them, nonetheless. Nick's enthusiasm for the sport, and for the success of others, was particularly infectious. On the car rides from school to swimming practice, Kenan relayed that his first coaching session of the day was always listening to his mentor, Nick. As an upstart underclassman, who at this point in his life wasn't as fast or talented as Nick, Kenan admired and respected that his friend had room in his life and in his heart for him. Kenan credits Nick, his "brother from another mother," for his swimming success, and for believing in Kenan when Kenan did not believe in himself.

Coach Andre said that many of the swimmers had their share of complaints and setbacks. Shoulder soreness was a common physical complaint and it wasn't met with much sympathy; in fact very few conditions were worthy of sympathy. He maintained this coaching style by design — to toughen the mental game of his athletes and to assure continuous progress. Coach Andre's response to most complaints was "get back to training, and train harder." However, he did know when a young swimmer needed to rest an injury. Sometimes swimmers, including Nick, laid off the weights and were seen only kicking to rest their shoulders, or performing some other modified workout. The beauty of modified workouts is that they were exceedingly boring, and when Nick was faced with them, his shoulders quickly healed.

At other times, the swimmers would beg for shorter distances in workouts, such as intervals of 50 meters. "Fifties" as they are called, are a sprinter's paradise. They are short and sweet; speed and rest. However, Coach Andre's practices rarely included 50s unless the team was preparing for competition. Coach Andre's philosophy was "50s do not prepare you for college." While this was Nick's favorite distance, he rarely got to practice this distance in his midseason training. But at swim meets at all times of the year, Nick often competed in 50s in all four strokes.

Nick was having a stellar junior year of high school swimming, enjoying both Coach Andre and Coach Lauren. His relationship with Coach Lauren was growing closer, and with guidance from both, he felt well prepared for the 2016 district, regional and state championships. Nick easily advanced through the district qualifying.

Swimming at regionals in 2016 was a high-stakes proposition for Nick. Ineligible to swim the previous year, and now completely invested in the sport, he wanted to show his teammates, his parents, and most importantly himself, that he had the ingredients of a champion. The complete package would be to qualify for states in both the 100- and the 50-yard free. Nick set his sights on this and nothing short of this. He knew that a high-place finish in both events would establish himself as the most dominant high school freestyle sprinter from South Florida.

My Mistakes Are My Strengths

At this year's regional qualifier, Nick first swam his favorite event: the 100-yard free. As the starting horn sounded, a different swimmer dove into the pool. Gone was the pumped-up, excited boy. As people watched Nick struggle to find his rhythm and pace, they wondered what was happening. The MSD spectator section of the stands became quiet. His final outcome in this race was devastating; it left him reeling. Not only did he swim a second slower than his best time, he also was disqualified. Nick had not been DQ'd in a race since he was a young swimmer. He was first crushed by his slow time, and then realized that because of the DQ, he had no chance to swim both freestyle events at states. However, in Nicholas Dworet style, this disappointment was quickly processed as he realized he needed to prepare for his next event, the 50-yard free. In a school essay written later, Nick described in his own words what happened:

Nicholas Dworet

Dr. Daon

August 30th, 2017

Period 8

My Mistakes Are My Strengths

The feeling I get when I'm standing behind the starting block and looking across the pool immerses me into the state of freedom. Telling myself that I'm going to conquer this race, and that this is my only chance to show the world who I am makes me feel like the greatest man alive. But those aren't the races I remember the most, the ones that protrude in my mind are usually the ones where I make a mistake and I mess up because those are the most important. My 100 freestyles at regionals in 2016, is one of those races that I still reminisce about and think to myself what I could have changed, But I will "Never let a stumble in the road, be the end of the journey."

Leading up to this race was countless early mornings and late nights that Consisted of swimming back and forth for thousands of meters looking at the dull concrete floor for more than six hours a day. This really gets in your head, all this training for one race does something to your mind psychologically. So, there I was, the beginning of high school swim season, more than prepared. I had the strength in my body but more importantly I had the strength in my mind. In the season, I dominated the dual meets and won every single race I swam. At districts I got first and at least one body length ahead of the person who came in second, but this was just child's play. The real meet I was preparing for was regionals, it was the meet that determines if you make it to states.

The 100 free was the 5th event, I had about an hour and half before I swam. When I hopped in the water to warm up, the water breezed off my skin it was almost like I was a bullet shooting at full speed. I got out of the water about 45 minutes before my race and went to sit down on my chair. I put my head down, and thought to myself "how many strokes are you going to take, how many breaths, how fast are you going to go". I visualized the race over and over in my mind. It was soon time to start heading toward the block. I took quick but concise steps it definitely looked like I knew what I was doing, unlike some other athletes who look like they got here by a luck of the draw. I got behind my block and felt butterflies build up in my stomach and sweat start to bubble onto my skin. I never like to tell myself before my race that I was nervous but I definitely was. The officials blow their whistle signaling to get onto the block I step up gracefully and get in my starting position. When they say "take your marks" I don't feel right I feel like I'm going to throw-up into the water I was thinking about how nervous I was and that was my first mistake.

The sound to start goes off and the second I hit the water my arms fall to my sides even though I should be in the streamline position. It felt like a big tsunami had engulfed my body, I struggled to get to the top of the water to take my first stroke. When I got on top and started swimming I pushed my body as much as I could, there was just no getting back, I couldn't catch up no matter how hard I tried. I got my hand on the wall and finished last, I also added one second to my best time which I was hoping to drop in this swim. I was devastated, but the worst was yet to come. I hopped out of the water and an official pulled me aside and told me "I'm sorry sir but we have to disqualify you for contemporary false start." My head spinning and my heart pounding I couldn't comprehend what had just happened. The word kept repeating in my head, over and over again like an alarm that you can't snooze. I walked back to the Stoneman Douglas tent recollecting my thoughts and going over what exactly happened. The meet went by like a breeze after that, heat after heat I sit there with a pale blank expression on my face. When the meet ended I went directly home and sat in my bed for hours staring into space asking myself how this could be. I woke up the next morning and I honestly felt relieved, I know that I shouldn't have exactly felt like this after flushing my whole season down the drain. But I thought to myself that morning that this wasn't the end but just a new beginning.

Mistakes in life are impossible to avoid so instead of dreading them accept them. I will never let any mistake be an obstacle for me, only a learning experiences. I'm so proud to say that I still go to practice every single day knowing that this could happen again. One thing that this incident has taught me is that life will rarely go the way you expect it to go all you can do is hope for the best, and be happy with what you get, and all I know is that I am.

If You Have a Lane, You Have a Chance

Nick's second event at regionals was the 50-yard free. On the heels of his 100-yard free failure, the "real Nick Dworet" showed up. Supporters who were there to watch the race recall it as a show-stopping epic swim. In swimming, there is an adage, "If you have a lane, you have a chance." This is exactly what was running through Nick's mind as he climbed onto the starting blocks. Seeded fifth in the final heat, Nick seemingly came out of nowhere, with explosive speed, to overtake the four faster qualifiers. He placed first by a mere four one-hundredths (.04) of a second. Kyle Oliver, who attended a different high school, years later still described with excitement what he watched from the pool deck: "At the finish, everyone was cheering, and I raised my voice even higher. With joy I stood up, pumped my fist, and said 'magnum opus,' by far the best race I have ever seen, Olympics included. If the race had been held on land rather than in the pool, Nick would have shook the earth. There wasn't a dry eye in the house."

Oliver said that everyone knew Nick had it in him. "His talent showed up loud and clear," he said. Nick outpaced his teammates Tristan Celestin (fourth) and Guy Bogoslavsky (sixth). By placing first, Nick was guaranteed a berth at the state championships.

The week prior to the MSD swim team departing for the state championships, Nick and Kyle Jones were skateboarding in front of the Dworets' house. Their tricks got a little rough and competitive. Kyle fell and split his chin open. Annika was quick to determine Kyle needed stitches. She called the hospital emergency room where she worked and facilitated a visit for Kyle. Annika was especially firm when speaking to the doctor: "This boy has to swim in the state championships in one week. Please be sure his wound is taken care of properly so that he can swim." Kyle was in and out of the emergency room quickly, and within days he was ready to swim.

As the team traveled to the state championships, Nick would compete in the 50-yard freestyle as well as the boys' 200-yard freestyle relay. Nick had not swum an individual race at states before. Out of tradition, swimmers who qualified for individual events, had first dibs on seat position in the van ride with Coach Lauren. Nick, as usual, picked the front seat. Then there were alternates such as Kyle Jones, who got the leftover seats. Rarely did an alternate swim. Instead, they were usually relegated to the cheering section to support their friends. By the end of the selection process, the school van was packed full of luggage and excited teenagers.

States were held each year in Stuart, Fla., a more than two-hour ride north of MSD. For the drive, Nick loved sitting shotgun where he and Coach Lauren could share adult conversation peppered by "team talk" from the teammates seated behind them. Coach Lauren had great listening skills, and Nick felt safe sharing his thoughts and dreams with her. Even though he was only swimming one individual race at states, Nick was excited for his teammates, and especially for their relay. Nick's upbeat and positive attitude was infectious, and the drive seemed quick. The team was usually housed at an economical hotel, where the first excursion was to a convenience store. The boys stocked up on a variety of snacks and comfort food which for Nick meant Oreos, white Kit-Kats, and energy drinks. Sometimes the snack food was based upon superstition; some swimmers believe they cannot swim their best times without a favorite food consumed at a specific time either before or after a race. Oreos were Nick's superstition, a form of essential, race-winning nutrition.

However, meals were also an important part of the entire team's preparation. Following a strict budget, Coach Lauren would arrange for group dining. The International House of Pancakes was one favorite. Nick knew the menu by heart, including the all-you-can-eat pancake specials. Nick had no need for a menu; he had a predetermined idea of what to order. Nick had never met a menu item he didn't like, although the IHOP Swedish pancakes were inferior to his grandmother's. Nick still would order them occasionally. IHOP provided good value, and every swimmer found themselves full and satisfied before competing.

In 2016, the state championships were held one month after the regional qualifying meet. Swimming his only individual event, the 50-yard free, Nick for the first time broke the 22-second barrier. Nick clocked a 21.97 time in the preliminary heat to qualify 10th for the finals. The finals of this race consisted mostly of high school seniors. Nick, among one of the younger competitors, placed 12th. As planned, Nick also competed in the boys' 200-free relay. Tristan Celestin (swimming in his last state championships), Joey Wong, and Guy Bogoslavsky were Nick's teammates in this event. Nick recorded a split of 21.73 for his 50-yard anchor swim.

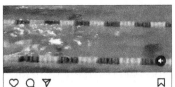

6,986 views · Liked by rememberingnickdworet

dnicm Had to catch up to get that win 👍👍 21.3 in the last leg of the 200 free relay (im the one with the light blue suit and pink cap I hoped in 2nd and then moved to first 🏆🏆) couldn't of done it without everyone espically @daria_chia of course 😊😊 well I really couldn't thank all of you guys that helped especially my whole team @tristancel @guybogo7 @joey #states #statesbound #douglas

View all 24 comments

October 30, 2016

To see Nick in action swimming in a preliminary relay to qualify for state competition scan the QR Code, and read his reaction in his own words from his Instagram account.

No Rest for the Weary

Pleased by his performance at states, Nick had no time to waste. He immediately returned to his training at TS Aquatics to continue his momentum in swimming and in life. Although the MSD water polo players would occasionally ask Nick if he were interested in a sprint or two, he politely turned them down. Now, he only wanted to swim. Club swimming continued throughout the winter of 2016 and into the spring of 2017, with Nick hardly missing an opportunity to compete throughout Florida. When not swimming on a weekend, his good grades had earned him the privilege to travel alone to Orlando to visit Daria. Daria recalled the early trips where Nick would ride the Greyhound bus and she would pick him up at the terminal, in a strange part of town, at all hours of the day and night. As the packed bus unloaded and she looked for Nick, the first thing Daria would notice was his big smile and outstretched arms ready for a big hug. When they reunited, it seemed like they had been apart for an eternity, even if it had only been a week. Daria and Nick would spend the weekends studying, ordering pizza, and watching movies. Academics were still extremely important to Daria, who was accustomed to being an honor student most of her life. Nick, too, found academics to be important now, with dreams of swimming for a good college hinging upon every 10th of a point improvement in his GPA.

In early 2017, Nick participated in several club competitions in Florida. He dominated his events. At the Naples Open, Nick swam an astounding seven individual events, never placing lower than 10th place against a large open field of men of any age. His best event was the 50 free where he was third among 35 competitors. Nick also placed well in the butterfly events, and the 100-yard backstroke. He was now showing momentum in the pool and at school. Many credited Daria with being a positive influence in his life, and a critical part of his success.

On Valentine's Day 2017, Nick wrote the following social media post:

"Today is a day not about giving items to each other but showing your love for one another, I am so thankful every single day to have such a wonderful and amazing girlfriend and today is the day to just look back and appreciate that. Appreciate all the people who you love and who love you back because that is what Valentine's Day really represents. I know we couldn't be together for this day Daria but I can't wait to celebrate with you this weekend I love you so much my princess! Forever & Always. Happy Valentines Day to everyone and I hope you had an astounding day just like I have."

As Nick's junior year was coming to a close, swimming competitions in Florida began to migrate to long course 50-meter pools. The transition was cumbersome, but like most young swimmers, Nick quickly adapted to the change. In May 2017, Nick had two good local meets. By placing fourth in the 200 IM at the Coral Springs Invitational, Nick demonstrated a rare versatility in the sport, an attribute which is valued by college scouts. Later in the summer, just before departing for Sweden, Nick had great performances at two prestigious local meets. At a meet on July 31, Nick caught a glimpse of his dreams. His times in the 50- and 100-meter free qualified him for the Swedish Jr. National Team, and also for USA Swimming Futures, elevating him to an elite status on two continents. The Futures level of swimming is just below the junior nationals; only two higher levels separate competitors from the U.S. Olympic trials. In Sweden, Nick was only one level away from national team qualifying, which in three years could position him for the Swedish Olympic trials.

Sweden Homecoming

Nick was looking forward to the annual trip this year more than ever because Daria was coming along to experience the joy of Sweden firsthand. Nick couldn't wait to introduce his girlfriend to his extended family. Annika and Mitch had lined up a swim team in Sweden where Nick could train. Nick worked out almost daily with the team. He became familiar with the work ethic and speed of his Swedish peers. Many of the swimmers were on the Swedish Junior National Team, and older swimmers were preparing to try out for the national team. Nick had an eye-opening experience swimming there because he saw for himself that he could keep pace and could qualify for the national team system in Sweden. His dream was within reach. This summer experience was a tangible roadmap for Nick to envision qualifying for the Olympics in the future. While he was still young in the sport, Nick saw that he could do it, and from then on, he made up his mind that he would do it. Annika and Mitch said this was a watershed moment for their son.

During their first weekend in Sweden, the family traveled to an international track and field event in Gothenberg where they watched Nick's cousin Ida compete. She participated in the long jump, 100-meter sprint, and the high jump. From there, they drove to Borås to view the Swedish National Team swimming competition. Nick was eager to see high-caliber competition in Sweden for the first time. He also met Sarah Sjöstrom, one of his idols. Sjöstrom is a four-time Olympian, and the most famous Swedish swimmer of the modern Olympic era. A photo was taken of Nick and Sarah together, which became one of his treasured keepsakes.

On their second weekend in Nora, Nick, Daria, and Annika competed in the traditional Utmaningen triathlon. For Nick, this was a repeat event. He was excited for a rematch with the swimmer who had beaten him in the swimming stage two years earlier. Nick wanted to be the first one out of the water this time. For Daria and Annika, the triathlon was a new experience. The Americans, each in their own way, had trained for this event. Daria won the swimming stage of the race. Her finish made a front-page headline: "The woman who traveled farthest, is first out of the water."

Although Daria's lack of familiarity with Swedish prevented her from reading the story, her picture spoke a thousand words about her accomplishment, and to her proud parents at home in the United States. For this race, Daria borrowed a well-worn bike from Nick's uncle. Annika borrowed a low-tech bike with malfunctioning gears, but she was able to pass Daria on the downhill portion of the bike ride. Later, Daria passed Annika back on the final running stage. Nick, although determined to be first out of the water, was again second. He later learned his competitor was a high-level Swedish National Team swimmer, who was at least five years Nick's senior. Nick, however, got his revenge, beating the same competitor in the running portion of the race, and therefore beating him overall. The next day, Nick's supposed training for this triathlon was revealed when again he could hardly walk due to sore legs. Gravity was not Nick's friend.

Sightseeing in Stockholm was another highlight of the trip. Nick and Daria went to the most-visited museum in Scandinavia, called the Vasa. The museum contains the largest fully intact 17th-century ship that has ever been salvaged. The 64-gun warship Vasa sank on her maiden voyage in 1628. Over 300 years later, the ship was rescued from the ocean floor, and painstakingly reassembled into a museum. After visiting the Vasa, the family visited an ice bar. Nearly every part of the bar was constructed of ice, including the walls, ceiling, seats, tables, and even the beverage glasses. While Mitch and Annika enjoyed a cocktail, the teenagers, sipping sodas, were becoming increasingly chilled. The family then realized they were wearing open-toe shoes — perfect for a summer day in Sweden, but not a visit to a below-zero, freezing bar. Cold and tired, and always hungry, they returned to Nora.

A trip to Nora is not complete without a cookout on the island in Lake Nörjason. Daria now understood the family tradition and memories made there. The roasted hot dogs and campfire were exceptional this year. Grandpa Nils fell much farther behind Nick in his customary swim race from the platform to shore. "There's no catching that boy, anymore," he announced.

 *To see the cousins and Daria jump off the platform into the lake, open this QR code.*

 *To see Nick do an encore backflip off the platform, open this QR code.*

As the Persson family gathered for the last time to say farewell to their American relatives, each member hugged one another and said, "Hej då" for "goodbye." Nick had become a changed young man on this trip. As he embraced his relatives, he contemplated the meaning of "Hej då."

Nick said to himself, "Never, ever, goodbye forever. Hello to our future. Bring it on."

The end of the vacation to Sweden came quickly, and Nick and Daria knew that it meant their separation would soon begin again. But for the long plane ride home, they nestled together with fond memories of their beautiful Scandinavian trip, each with hopes for a banner year in the United States.

CHAPTER NINE: BREASTSTROKE

"Love is just a word until someone comes along to give it meaning."

– Nicholas Dworet

Once the airplane from Sweden touched down in the United States, the summer of 2017 was over. Days later, in what seemed like a whirlwind, Daria drove away in her overstuffed car for her sophomore year of college. Nick stood in the driveway until Daria's car was long out of sight, missing her already.

Daria and Nick could endure separation once again because both had goals. Daria wanted to continue performing well in college, and Nick was looking forward to his senior year of high school. Just three short years earlier he had lost sight of his future, and college was not even a possibility with his failing grades. But now, Nick was aiming for higher than a cumulative 3.0 GPA. He decided he wanted to go to college and major in business. His dreams hinged upon a mistake-free senior year. Nick knew he could and would be great, but the work ahead would be harder than ever in both the pool and the classroom. Nick decided to apply his competitive skills to this high-stakes period in his life.

Nick held a meeting with his parents to discuss his future college budget needs, complete with a detailed spreadsheet, aiming to make his future education financially less burdensome on their family, especially if he chose to go to school outside of Florida. Mitch and Annika caught a familiar look in Nick's eyes. It was the intense 1,000-mile stare of a champion, just like the stare Nick had before a race. "I'm going to get a swimming scholarship," Nick said. There would be no stopping him. In his mind, a full-ride scholarship was the only option. With pride and confidence, he hugged his tearful parents.

Over the past three years, Coach Lauren had developed a very special relationship with Nick and had seen her challenging "project" become a cherished leader. As classes commenced at Marjory Stoneman Douglas, Coach Lauren had some unfinished business with Nicholas Dworet. Nick and his parents didn't know it, until Coach Lauren called an unexpected meeting. Over the short but happy summer, she had a nagging and unsettling feeling in the back of her mind that revolved around Nick's level of commitment. Coach Lauren didn't question that Nick had commitment. She knew his potential was exceptional, but she didn't want Nick to have distractions which may cause mistakes in his senior year. Coach Lauren had discovered her ability to be a third parent, and now was her opportunity to gently insert herself into a very important time in Nick's life.

Even though Daria was over 200 miles away at college, she too was included in this meeting by phone to assure that all who loved Nick knew what distraction-free meant. Nick needed to capture every chance for success and to assure optimum exposure to college scouts. Coach Lauren had noticed Daria's discipline toward academics and toward her new sport of crew and asked the couple to replicate this discipline in Nick's studies and training. For example, Nick woke early most mornings to call Daria to remind her to go to crew practice. Daria committed to do the same for Nick.

Mitch and Annika also reinforced the importance of Nick's college search process. They discussed his study habits, his nutrition and sleep habits, and lastly his social habits. Coach Lauren knew intuitively that if she could get Nick to write down his goals, she could harness all his energy into rare greatness, of which she was thrilled to be a part.

Upon leaving the meeting, Coach Lauren and Nick set up an additional meeting for private goal-setting, which was held the next week. It was here where they intimately defined the future times he could aspire to in the pool, and the effort required to attain those goals. Nick erased his goals a few times, rewriting them and carefully contemplating the possibilities of both reaching, and not reaching his goals. He decided to fortify the process by adding the words "I will let nothing stand in my way." At the very bottom he wrote, "Train harder." All of Nick's goal times were for long-course meters (LCM); it is the distance swum at the Olympics. In other words, LCM is all that mattered. Nick's 2019 goals were aligned with times needed to qualify for the Swedish Junior National Team. He was a man with a plan.

-I want to become a Swedish olympian and go to Tokyo 2020 to compete for my Country.
-I will give All I have in my body and my mind to Achieve the goal I have set. I will train as hard as I can in and out of the water. Even on my hardest days I swear to give it my all, and I will let nothing stand in my way.
-Dates

1/31/2018	3/09/18
50 Free LCM: 24.53	50 free LCM: 23.99
100 Free LCM: 53.79	100 Free LCM: 52:00
200 Free LCM: 2:03.95	200 Free Lcm: 1:55.81
400 Free LCM: 4:31.15	400 Free LCM: 4:11.50
200 IM LCM: 2:23.61	200 IM LCM: 2:11.00

2019
50 Free LCM: 22.99
100 Free LCM: ~~51.50~~ 50.00!!
200 Free LCM: 1:53.99
400 Free LCm: 4:00.00
200 IM LCm: 2:07.00

-Train harder

Now prepared with his first serious written goals, Nick safely taped them to the wall by the side of his bed.

Nick stared at his goals constantly. He memorized each word and recited his goal statement to himself during workouts. His goals were the first thing he saw as he awoke, and the last thing he read before dozing off at night; they became seared into his consciousness.

Nick and Daria also had a mutual goal to grow their love. They made the most of long weekends and holidays together. One time, they went to a painting class where they each painted an elephant. When the weekend ended and they returned to their respective homes, they exchanged the paintings so Nick could view Daria's painting and Daria could display Nick's. Another time, in Coral Springs, Nick and Daria decided to go to the movies. They stopped at a dollar store to buy candy. Nick recognized the cashier as a young man who had recently dropped out of MSD. The cashier is the person who later would take Nick's life. This was the only known interaction Nick had with him prior to Feb. 14, 2018. There were times, too, when the love birds would use social media to boost each other's spirits. One time, Nick wrote a poem to Daria:

> *If you're alone I'll be your shadow*
> *If you want to cry I'll be your shoulder*
> *If you're not happy I'll be your smile*
> *If you need me I'll always be there*
> *I love you Daria forever and always.*

Going Places As Fast As He Can

Meanwhile back at the pool, with Nicholas Dworet as captain, the MSD swim team was poised for a banner year. High school swimming created a team atmosphere in a sport which usually is deemed an individual sport. Nick enjoyed watching his team succeed more than himself. He was a consummate overcheerer, known to cheer consistently and loudly for his teammates until he became hoarse. Nick knew what humility was. It's not thinking less of yourself, it is thinking of yourself less.

The format of this high school swimming season hadn't changed from the past. Initially there were dual meets. The competition in these meets was inconsistent, but Nick treated each and every race with seriousness.

The carrot at the end of the stick was the same three final swim meets: districts, regionals, and state championships.

At the unrelated Broward County Athletic Association meet in October 2017, Nick placed first in the 50-yard free, recording a time of 21.77. He also placed first in the 100-yard free, recording a searing 47.87. Each were personal records. Nick was the second person in recent history to place first in two events at this large regional meet. At the district qualifiers, Nick swept the 50- and 100-freestyle events. The following week at the regional qualifier, Nick swam a slightly slower 50 free, and a PR 100 free (47.53), to secure his position in both events at states.

Nick was proud to be swimming his favorite events at the end of his high school career. Very few swimmers qualify for two individual events, and Nick was also grateful to swim his favorite race, the 100 free, after his debacle the prior year. Again, Nick and his teammates repeated their trek to Stuart. This time, his ride with Coach Lauren was peppered with business talk. She listened intently as Nick related anecdotes from reading "Rich Dad, Poor Dad." She noticed Nick's enthusiasm for business was nearly as great as his enthusiasm for swimming. This year, Guy would be Nick's roommate. Guy was one of the alternates who came along to possibly swim the 200 yard-free relay.

Guy had been roommates with Nick before and given his experience, he took to overseeing all the elements necessary for his friend to succeed. This included assistance with shaving nearly every hair off Nick's body and assuring that Nick had the right kind of nutrition and sleep. They had some light fun because Guy also enjoyed rap music. The music sounded better as it got louder. They shared their love for the song "Almost Famous" by G-Eazy, and the music of many other artists, including Hi-Rez. The snacks were as plentiful as the laughs; lights were out early as planned. Guy even had to get Nick to stop FaceTiming with Daria. Guy said, "Nick and Daria were locked together, and only Daria had the key." The only serious moments were when Daria called. Nick's voice became different, calm and high-pitched. The music was turned down, or Nick left the room for a quiet place. They could talk for hours, but when Nick hung up, their room would return to normal: Nick and Guy's man cave.

Nick researched the best jammer suits for the state championships. He decided on the Mizuno GX Sonic III suit, worn by Olympian and world-record holder Caleb Dressel. At the world championships in 2017, Dressel broke the American record in the 50-meter butterfly, wearing this tight, magenta garment. It was rumored that this suit reduced resistance on the body by maintaining a flat posture. To do this, the suit supports muscles from the torso and hamstrings, binding the muscles toward the hips. Many believed that it improved a sprinter's kicking ability. Nick soon discovered that this exact suit was not yet available in the United States, so he searched worldwide until he could find one for sale. Nick located a seller in Japan, and ordered the suit on eBay.

Now owning the exact kind of magenta swimsuit worn by Dressel, Nick was prepared. Nick had exceptional individual results at the state championships. Nick now expected to regularly break 22.0 in the 50 free. In this final meet of his high school career, he recorded 21.62 which earned him 11th place amid a very competitive field. In the 100 free, Nick placed fifth with a personal record of 46.53. Following this race, a coach from the University of Tampa came over to speak with Nick. The coach had first contacted Nick's parents nearly a year earlier regarding his college plans. Nick's most noteworthy performance at his last state championships was his 20.99 split as anchor of the 200 free relay. For any 50-yard free sprinter, breaking the 21-second barrier is a tremendous feat. In total, Nick scored 20 points for Marjory Stoneman Douglas. At home in Nora, Grampa Nils and Grandma Birgitta were able to watch their grandson achieve this milestone through live streaming. Nick's success was a family success.

To see Nick's medal ceremony open the QR code.

To see Nick swim the 50 freestyle in a preliminary heat of this event, open the QR code.

Brother Time

Due to his regimented schedule, Nick and his younger brother Alex seemed to be spending less time together than they had in the past. Nevertheless, they had a respectful, mature relationship and enjoyed being together. Nick devised a plan, which soon became a routine. After dinner, he would ask his parents if he could take Alex to the store to buy something unimportant like Chapstick. The boys would take off in the Volvo, put the windows down, and play their favorite music. Once at the store, Nick would buy at least two packages of Oreos, sometimes more. Quickly returning to the car, they tore into one of the packages. Some people carefully pull apart Oreos and methodically eat the inside first, followed by the cookie wafers. Nick had no such method except to eat them as fast as he could. Alex could only eat about half a row while Nick could eat the rest of the package; sometimes faster than Alex. The unopened packages of Oreos were destined for an increasingly large secret hoard of cookies which were safely hidden in Nick's closet at home.

Longing for these fun and playful times together, the two boys went out after dinner frequently. These "necessary trips" also created an opportunity for Nick to teach Alex to drive. After safely leaving the supermarket, the boys would travel to the hills of Coral Springs to a quiet cul-de-sac named Northwest 45th Manor. It was here where the boys switched seats and Alex learned to drive. This was the exact location where Mitch had taught Nick to drive a few years earlier. Mitch and Nick also had to keep their driving lessons a secret from Annika, fearing her disapproval. As the happy brothers returned home with the "necessary item," they had to remember what it was they told their parents they needed to buy. The truth was that Oreos were always necessary; the empty packages were safely disposed of as Nick went straight to his room to stow away the unopened cookies. Several years later, when Mitch began to teach Alex to drive, he described him as a "quick learner who had exceptional driving skills from the get-go." The Dworet brothers knew how to keep secrets.

College Selection Time

Concurrent to Coach Lauren's out-of-the-pool "dry" coaching, Coach Andre, was exercising his own third-parent skills. For most swimmers who were seniors in high school, Coach Andre had a rule that they had to reach out to five colleges or universities to seek entry, as either a swimmer, a student, or both. Swimming in college was not a requirement for TS swimmers but applying and going to college was an expectation for most.

Coach Andre left the college selection process up to the swimmers, although many by now had relationships, friends, or formal inquiries that generated promising leads. Excited whispers of Nick's swimming abilities had passed through the lips of many college coaches, but those whispers were muted when they learned of his grades. Nick's grades kept most coaches from picking up the phone and calling him directly. So, Nick took it upon himself to seek out colleges which could provide him a great business education and a swimming coach to help him reach his dreams.

By the end of 2017, Nick's college search process was narrowed down to two schools, the University of Tampa, and the University of Indianapolis (UINDY). While he knew Indianapolis would be a logistical and financial challenge, Nick bonded with UINDY's coach, Jason Hite, from the very beginning. Also, UINDY trained periodically in Hawaii, which satisfied Nick's childhood fascination to visit Hawaii and finally meet a Humuhumunukunukuapuaa fish up close in the wild. Nick, however, gave the University of Tampa further consideration.

In September 2017, Nick and his family made a five-hour drive for a recruiting trip to the University of Tampa. Nick met with the coach and his prospective teammates and had a great impression of this beautiful school. Later one evening, the swimmers took Nick out alone to a party. This was not the evening of fun that Nick had expected; he may have thought he was going out to eat. This experience provided Nick a glimpse backward into his past and he registered it in his mind as he continued his college selection process.

On the long ride home, Mitch and Annika were surprised that Nick was not more enthusiastic about Tampa. The Tampa swimmers were excited that such a talented prospect was visiting their school. They were nice and wanted Nick. Also, Mitch and Annika favored Tampa because it was close to home and closer to Daria, which made it a practical choice.

Nick, though, was following his intuition. Even given some of the logical arguments for considering Tampa, Nick became even more curious about Indianapolis. He decided that Tampa was not the exact fit. As a result, Nick scheduled a trip to the University of Indianapolis.

When it came time to visit the UINDY Greyhounds, Nick traveled by himself. Coach Hite remembered Nick as full of energy and life when he arrived on campus. Coach Hite said from the first moment, Nick was meant to be a Hound. Even the colors of Indianapolis were the same as those of Marjory Stoneman Douglas. The meeting between prospective coach and swimmer was key to Nick's decision. Nick found Coach Hite to be similar to Coach Andre, in that he too had been a standout swimmer. As a student-athlete, in the mid-1990s, Hite was an All-American athlete and an Academic All-American at Drury University in Missouri. Jason swam the individual medley, butterfly, and distance freestyle. He was the captain of the swim team in 1997.

As the swimmer and coach came to know each other, discovery of the parallels in their lives continued to accrue. There were minute differences as well. For example, Jason had grown up with snow, and he was able to watch Nick enjoy snow for the first time.

"It was the first time he'd seen snow, [the] first and only time he [had] made a snowball, and a snow angel. It was a neat experience for him," Hite said. "Like I said, he loved every minute of it. Even though he was just here for a weekend, we felt very connected to him. He was a very vibrant, energetic young man and he really fit in very well with everything we were doing here."

Coach Hite also knew that Nick had overcome several obstacles through his love of swimming.

"He realized swimming was a vehicle he could use to turn his whole life around. ...When he came here, he was nonstop questions, nonstop smiles," Hite recalled. "When you see someone who has made changes in their life and their swimming times are also progressing quickly, that's the kind of person you want to be part of your family and we knew Nick was going to be a great part of the group."

The positive feelings were mutual. Nick had found his home as a Hound. Shortly after this trip, Nick would learn that he had earned a scholarship to UINDY. In other words, Nick had accomplished his goal of earning his way into college.

You Can Do It

Late one evening, as Nick was drifting off to sleep, his phone rang. Ethan Searle was on the other end, and he sounded distressed. They hadn't spoken in a few months because Nick didn't want to disturb Ethan, who was a freshman at Boston College. Academics had always been Ethan's priority, and Nick knew not to distract him. What swimming meant to Nick, academics meant to Ethan.

Ethan shared with Nick he was concerned about his first round of final exams, and Ethan was very upset that he may possibly fail a class. Failure had never been an option for Ethan, and Nick was a safe confidante he could entrust with his fears. Ethan was scared and needed advice from his lifelong friend. Nick told Ethan, "You are the smartest, most capable person I know. If anyone could pull out a passing grade, it is YOU, Ethan. I totally believe in you Ethan."

Nick encouraged his friend to look at the positive side of his exams, and to study and do all that he could do to pass.

Repeatedly, Nick said, "I totally believe in you Ethan, you can do it. This is a temporary lapse in confidence; a result of overstudying and a lack of sleep." He encouraged Ethan to get a good night's rest and to call again. As Nick hung up the phone, he had no doubt that Ethan would pass with flying colors and hoped that Ethan knew himself that he would pass. Ethan did not call again, and Nick believed that was a good sign. Just a few weeks later at Christmas dinner, Ethan told Nick in private: "Nick, you kept me in college. You kept me from quitting. You kept me from failing. I passed this difficult semester, only because of your unwavering faith in me when I didn't even have faith in myself."

Ethan said that Nick was always a positive influence on him in life, and that he always had time to talk. "Nick was a selfless believer in those he loved."

After practice at TS Aquatics, Nick would sometimes visit Alex, Daria's mom. These visits could be spontaneous and were always welcomed by Alex; she and Nick had a special relationship. He was the son she never had.

One afternoon, while driving toward her house, he called her to see if she was home. She didn't answer. Even though she always welcomed Nick, Alex wasn't up for a visit because she felt her house was not up to her own housekeeping standards. She didn't want Nick to see a messy house.

A few minutes later, Nick called again, and Alex answered.

Nick said: "Alex, hi, are you home?"

Alex replied: "No, Nick, not now, but I will be in a while."

Nick replied, "I hope you're up for a visit because I know you're home. I'm parked in your driveway behind your car."

Alex, by now laughing, opened the front door. She's certain he didn't notice the condition of the house. She fed him one of his favorite snacks, and they had a nice conversation before he headed home.

At the conclusion of the high school swimming season, club swimming continued with a vengeance. There was no rest for the weary, and Coach Andre resumed workouts with a fury. Even though Nick had been able to taper (a gradual reduction in workouts that increases rest) for state championships, he hardly had time to bask in the success of his last high school competition. College was awaiting and tough work began the week after he returned from states. For swimmers, the period between January and June is considered a prime training opportunity, with a summer taper usually occurring after June, depending upon which championships lie ahead. For Nick, it would be the Futures races. Coach Andre's punishing workouts were familiar to Nick, who welcomed the opportunity to work hard again; his enthusiasm was ever present.

In January 2018, Nick's first meet after states was the Naples Open. A tired, sore boy showed up to compete, which is all part of the plan. Coach Andre wanted to see his swimmers improve while they were sore and tired, amid hard training, so that later when they rested, their improvements were dramatic. After creating an irreparable tear in his Mizuno jammers, Nick used an alternate suit and swam eight individual events at this meet, including the 500- and 1,000-yard free events. Nick now regularly broke the 1-minute per one-hundred standard. His time in the 500 was 4:45.49, and he clocked 9:55.18 in the 1000. Nick placed in the top three in most of the events he swam. His performance was outstanding given his return to hard training. The day after this meet, Nick was back in the pool training. Nothing could stop him.

A Safe Place

Also about this time, which was Nick's final semester of high school, he began to read "Think and Grow Rich," by Napoleon Hill. During lunch periods when Coach Lauren was conducting peer counseling, Nick and Guy would quietly enter the back of her classroom. Nick and Guy were the only swimmers who had permission to relax here, and before eating lunch they sometimes cleared boxes and materials accumulated on the well-worn sofa. Then they would plop down and sink into its soft folds, eager for food. Sometimes Nick would lay flat on his back with his feet on the armrest, with the small paperback resting upon his chest. Other times, the boys would quietly share their special place for lunch, not reading or doing much of anything, besides being friends.

As Nick became more enthralled with "Think and Grow Rich," it began to shape his thinking and his conversations. Reading this book slowly and carefully in the safe space of Coach Lauren's classroom, Nick thought of Daria and their future. One of the book's passages struck a chord. The book's author found that by reviewing the achievements of hundreds of successful men, "There was the influence of a woman's love on the back of every one of them."

Nick reflected upon all the influential women is his life. He understood that his love was maturing, and that Daria was likely to be the woman to provide "love on his back" forever. As he gave it more thought though, he realized that Hill lived in days gone by. "Think and Grow Rich" was written in 1937. Had Hill written this book in the present, Daria would never influence Nick from behind; rather she would travel by his side, as an equal on this wild journey. For an instant, this revelation caused Nick to love Daria even more, if that were possible.

CHAPTER TEN: FREESTYLE

"Then there they were...... the last words."

– A.D. Aliwat

On Jan. 27, 2018, TS Aquatics hosted their second annual awards banquet. Nick was recognized as the most improved swimmer. Coach Andre spoke about Nick's transformation into a formidable competitor. Nick's progress had been stratospheric, a remarkable short journey to this point, certainly to last well into his future. The slide presentation honoring the swimmers contained an inordinate number of pictures of Daria. Many wondered if she were on the team, too. The ever-loyal Daria was there frequently as a spectator to see Nick compete. Never far from one another, Daria and Nick were often photographed together. While driving to the banquet, Annika and Mitch asked Nick a few questions. They learned that he was going to be a speaker. Annika asked him if he had prepared a speech. Nick said, "No, it's all up here," pointing to his head. Nick was to be the last program speaker, as he would honor the coaches following the awards to the swimmers. Nick had prepared himself to speak during all the hours of contemplation in the pool over the past 18 months. His speech was rock solid. No notes. As Nick took to the lectern, his champion talking skills showed up. Nick delivered a beautiful, extemporaneous speech, complementing the qualities of each coach.
He generated a beautiful, positive energy in the room. At the end, his teammates gave him as standing ovation. Nick's speech was a highlight of the evening.

Signing Day

Just a week later, on Feb. 4, Marjory Stoneman Douglas was hosting signing day for each student-athlete who would be going to college to play their respective sport. Each student-athlete signs his or her letter of intent. This was an exceptionally happy day for the Dworet family. When it came time for Nick to sign his letter of intent to swim for the University of Indianapolis, Mitch, Annika, and Alex formed a tight semicircle around Nick, who was adorned in UINDY gear. As he signed, Nick silently read from a short script, reminding him to hold his pen up high, to smile, and to prepare a meaningful signature. In fact, his letter had been signed in private, days before. Nicholas Dworet was the first child of this generation, on either side of the family, to earn an athletic scholarship to college.

To view Nick's signing ceremony, access this QR code.

The same day, Carlos Vasquez signed with Penn State. The two friends had made it to college together. Coach Andre posted on social media, "Well done, gentlemen, well-deserved and we can't wait to see what you can achieve in your futures." Also, Nick's childhood friend, Alexandra Greenwald, had received a gymnastics scholarship to Iowa, her parent's alma mater. When she learned Nick would be swimming for UINDY, Alexandra knew that her moment of pride was Nick's and vice versa. The memories from years ago where they pledged to one another to be the best that they could be, on the little blanket as their parents ran a 5K, had come true.

On Feb 8, 2018, Coach Andre posted on social media: "Your

competition is with yourself. Push harder." The weekend of Feb. 10, 2018, was a busy one at the Dworet household. Grandmother Barbara Dworet was visiting for a few weeks in preparation to move to a new home. Barbara always enjoyed watching Nick swim, and on this particular weekend, she came along with the family to all the places they needed to be. There were two swim meets, one Saturday and one on Sunday, as well as brother Alex's birthday celebration. Additionally, Daria was in town to celebrate Valentine's Day. At the end of the weekend, Daria traveled back to school.

On Saturday, Feb. 10, Nick swam his first long-course meet of the season at the Long Course Sectional Qualifier. Coach Andre set expectations at this meet to be reasonably low. The reasons were because of the return to hard training, and the fact that competition was switching from the short, 25-yard pool to a 50-meter pool, always a cumbersome transition. Nick now had his written goals within sight. While posting few personal records here (and not expecting to), Nick had solid performances in four events. Nick nearly broke his goal times in two events: the 200-meter free and the 200 IM. Coach Andre and Nick were satisfied with his showing.

On Sunday, Feb. 11, Nick swam his last short-course meet of the season. It was called the Coral Springs Open Invitational Championship. This meet was a large South Florida competition which attracted swimmers up to age 19 from all over the state. There was a boys' division and a girls' division; age groups were not in play. In the 200 free, Nick placed first out of a field of 100 swimmers. Diego placed third, and Nick's pal Kenan placed 15th. Nick also swam the 100-yard IM, placing fourth. Nick's buddy Carlos Vasquez dropped over 10 seconds from his entry time to place second in this event; many other TS Aquatics swimmers placed in the top 10.

Nick's final event was one of his favorites: the 50-yard free. By just a few hundredths of a second, Nick outtouched his teammates and training partners Carlos and Diego, to resoundingly win this event among a field of 153 competitors. It was now undisputed that Nick was one of the finest sprinters of his generation from South Florida. After much driving, competition and family time, the last, happy celebration of the weekend was on Sunday evening when the family went to a local buffet where they celebrated Alex's 14th birthday. Buffets were always a good choice with this crowd, and the weekend ended on a high note.

Good Night, Mamma

On Monday, Feb. 12, Nick stayed unusually long after practice and talked with the younger swimmers until late into the evening. Many related that Nick's willingness to listen and to talk was inspiring beyond belief, and that this impromptu meeting caused them to recommit to the sport. Nick was cold, tired, and hungry when he went home. However, he was also missing his mother. Annika had worked a 12-hour shift that day and was sound asleep. Knowing how hard her job was, Nick didn't usually disturb Annika when she was sleeping. Tonight was different. Nick entered her bedroom and woke her up from a sound sleep. Thinking something was awry, she asked if everything was all right. He said, "Oh yes, Mamma. I just missed you and wanted to hear the sound of your voice."

Tuesday, Feb. 13 was an ordinary day for Nick. He had school, swimming and FaceTimed with Daria; just like most any other day. That evening, Nick firmed up his new roommate at UINDY, a fellow freshman swimmer.

Feb. 14, 2018, also began as an ordinary day at the Dworets' home. Annika felt rushed getting the boys out the door to school. She and Mitch ran through their schedule, which involved meeting Nick after school at a shopping center across the street so he could quickly reach the car and get to swimming practice on time. Nick was wearing his favorite light blue, long-sleeved T-shirt. As food, clothes, backpacks, and other items were collected, Nick and his brother made it to the car and Mitch drove them to school. They barely arrived on time. Nick messaged Daria with a sweet Valentine's message. Alexandra Greenwald would see Nick during two classes that morning. She was among Nick's oldest friends, and as they greeted one another with familiar grace, she relished their special friendship. In the afternoon, they would go their separate ways, each to different classes.

2:15 PM

Nick's last class, Holocaust studies, was in the freshman building, across the hall from his brother, Alex. Nick was quite interested in what the teacher was discussing this day because although the subject of the Holocaust was horrific, her questions involved sports. As she was leading up to a lecture about the 1936 Olympics, the teacher asked the class the following question:

"Does anyone know who Adi Dassler is?"

The classroom was silent. No one knew the answer. Nick raised his and said: "He is the founder of Adidas and his brother made Pumas."

The teacher was surprised and uttered "correct answer." In the four years she had taught this popular class no student had ever known the answer; that was, up until Nicholas Dworet.

The teacher asked Nick, "How did you know that?" It was 2:21 pm.

A murderous intruder had entered the hallway at this moment in the discussion. He went door to door on the first floor and shot through the windows of the classrooms. At 2:22 pm, before he was able to answer his teacher's question, Nicholas Dworet was shot in Room 1214 and died instantly. By 2:28pm, the shooter had walked away.

As long as life exists on earth there will be evil. It is insidious and indiscriminate. It is timeless. Evil surrounds us. Or, to quote Nick himself:

EPILOGUE

2:27 PM, February 14, 2018

The shooting stopped. Seventeen students and school personnel were dying or dead. Seventeen others, including Alex Dworet, Nick's brother, were wounded. Thousands of students, teachers, family members, and those in the community were traumatized, and shall forever be traumatized.

The Village

The village came together like no other to surround the Dworet family and hundreds of others needing support in the North Broward County, Florida, area. To this day, the village continues to lock arms, surrounding, protecting, and loving the Dworets and others.

Nicole

On Feb. 14, 2018, Nicole Nilsson left her own family, consisting of three children and her husband, to come to the Dworets' home and comfort the family for a prolonged period of time. She took care of the entire grieving household. Nicole managed visitors, the reporters who surrounded their home, as well as law enforcement inquiries. Nicole answered the phone and the front door continually. She also assisted with the delicate tasks related to Nick's service. Nicole coordinated the travel and lodging for the Dworets' Swedish family members. Nicole did anything for the family that a loving relative would do.

Nick Swims Forever

Nick has been laid to rest in three bodies of water – the Pacific Ocean, the Atlantic Ocean and Lake Norasjön. He shall swim forever.

Graduation

On June 3, 2018, Alexandra Greenwald walked for Nick during the graduation ceremony for Marjory Stoneman Douglas. Some of Nick's fellow classmates held hands and sang "Shine," a song written by MSD students in the aftermath of the shooting.

Rapper Hi Rez

In August 2018, Hi-Rez released "We Want Change," a song he created in Nick's memory. The song has over 5 million YouTube views; and is a soulful yet commercial success for Nick's cousin.

To see Hi-Rez perform this moving song, scan the code.

Dragonfly

A professional in the healing profession once said that Nick may be represented by a living dragonfly in our current world. When dragonflies visit, some believe it is Nick visiting.

Nick's Legacy

The Nicholas Dworet Memorial Fund has been established to support swimmers of all levels. Its main focus is to assist college-bound swimmers with scholarships. For further information, please visit: www.NDMF.org.

100% of the proceeds of this book are donated to the Nicholas Dworet Memorial Trust.

You can also visit the Nicholas Dworet Memorial Fund by accessing this QR code.

To learn more about this book, including media and public discussion and book signings, please access this QR code, which links you to the Soul of a Swimmer website.

ACKNOWLEDGEMENTS

The Village

First, we thank the expansive village, an extraordinary group of neighbors and friends who opened their arms and their hearts to me. I especially thank Joe Chiarella, Sue Colton, Alexandra Greenwald, Mark Greenwald, Kristine Hiler, Leif Nilsson, Nicole Nilsson, Ethan Searle, and Kathy Searle. Many thanks to the other members of the village; you know who you are.

My School of Fish

Thank you to two of my oldest fish friends and lane mates, Leslie Vuoso and Linda Otos, who both relished each word I've spoon-fed them; we've shared the language of swimming and the language of life now for over 50 years. To Gail Musk, my college roommate, who like an Oreo is so soft on the inside. Thank you for the mom-of-boys perspective.

Thanks to Marlys Cappert, Michele DeStefano, Debbie Eisinger, Peter Horwitz, Deborah Rosenbaum, and Brian Webb.

A very special thanks to my Swim Fort Lauderdale teammates and to the rest of my school of fish.

Nick's School of Fish

Thanks to Tristan Celestin, the only interviewee who actually fell for my last question: "How about we take a swim in the ocean after our interview?" Thanks for being such a good sport.

Thanks to David Blanco, Guy Bogoslavsky, Geoffrey Hayman, Justin Irwin, Kenan Kocoglu, Kyle Jones, Alexio Musleh, Kyle Oliver, Joymarie Puskasdi, and Carlos Vasquez.

Lastly, to Daria Chiarella, a woman whom Nick could not love more. Thank you.

Our Coaches

To Coach Lauren Rubenstein, a resilient hero to countless swimmers. Thank you for your steadfast commitment to Marjory Stoneman Douglas High School, where you continue to teach and coach to this day.

To Coach Jason Hite, thank you for making Nick's dreams yours.

To Coach Andre Bailey, for once I get the last word here; great swimmers can be great coaches. But, it must begin with being a great person. You are a great person through and through.

Also, thank you, to Coach Marty Hendrick, who reawakened my swimmer's soul. Lastly, thank you to Coach Stuart Horwitz, a coach like no other, a landlubber who swam the distance with me beautifully, side by side, shoulder to shoulder, sharing the language of swimming. I couldn't have done it without you.

The Spectators

A very special thanks to Laurie Marachwinski, Ivonne Schmid, and Brent Rutemiller, who early on understood the importance of this project.

Thanks to Jose Arango, Barry Ger, Joseph Collum, Chantal Govaerts, Debbie Harnden, Cindy Kramer, Knyvett Lee, Jerry Madden, Mike McCann, Bill Moore, Teri Moore-Morgan, Nancy Myers, Kelly Perroni, David and Sara Jane Rose, Melody Saleh, Allison Scheflow, and Frank, Jana and Max Yanover.

Thanks to our Hawaii contingent: Michael and Claire D'Dario, Dave Hafele, Kimokeo Kapahulehua, Mark Libre, Lisa Mann, Ron Panzo, Anthony Pfluke, Brad and Gina Nicolai, and Monique Rice. Many thanks to Kim Snyder and team, for their interest in this project and for their unwavering support for the Parkland community. Special thanks to Michael Nicloy of Nico 11 Publishing & Design. Things happen for a reason, and you were there to shepherd me at the right time. Thanks to CG Sports Publishing for finally making this project a reality; we are grateful for you believing in us. It has been a pleasure to work with all of you, including Cejih Yung, Matthew Amerlan, Holly Neumann, P.K. Daniel, and Nicole Wurtele.

Our Family

Many thanks to Nick's grandparents, Birgitta and Nils Persson. Thanks to Nick's aunt and uncles Ulrika Pettersson, Niklas Pettersson, Goran Persson, and Inger Persson. Thank you to Nick's cousins, Ida and Elin Pettersson, and Joakim Persson and Daniel Persson. On the Albano side of the family, first, to my daddy, Peter Albano, an astounding author, and my lifelong inspiration. Thanks to Lisa and John Hall, and Teri and Rob Hall. Also, many thanks to Laura Albano; it was glorious to watch you love the Dworets as your own. Thank you to Carolyn Cann, my first and finest sounding board. Thank you to George-Henry Cann-Gudat for his young adult perspective, and to Carrie Sue Hof, thank you for listening. Most importantly, to my husband George Cann. Thank you for coming along with me on this awesome and wild swim called life. I am eternally grateful to you for your love and support of my swimmer's soul. Without the beautiful love story of Mitch and Annika Dworet there never would have been such an extraordinary human being named Nicholas Dworet. But, you created two extraordinary sons. Thank you for raising such an exceptional young adult, Alexander Dworet, Nicholas' younger brother. I thank each of the Dworets for believing in me, envisioning this dream, and for having the fortitude to assist me in telling Nick's story. You faced unbearable pain in this process so that Nick can live on through *Soul of a Swimmer*.

Finally, to Nick,

I believe we met somewhere, some place in the sea. I held you as best I could as water passed through my hands. I looked up at the morning sky and said, "What the hell is water?" and we swam on. Hej då for now.

Love, Fyshy

Pictured above: Carla Albano, Photo courtesy of George Cann

ABOUT CARLA ALBANO

Carla Albano grew up in Southern California in the 1960s and 1970s. She began swimming competitively at age 7 in a region considered to be a hotbed for elite swimming. Carla enjoyed a modest level of success competing in the pool and open-water venues.

In 1976, as a senior in high school, Carla was the breaststroker on a medley relay which broke the California Interscholastic Federation record, an accomplishment which stood for nearly two decades.

Also in 1976, Carla qualified as the first woman ocean lifeguard in Long Beach, California. That year, she became a breaststroker for California State University, Long Beach, women's varsity swim team. She swam for CSULB for two years, retiring from competitive swimming in 1978.

Over the next four decades, Carla attended college and law school. She was admitted to the California Bar in 1995. Carla had a long career in healthcare. She moved with her husband to Fort Lauderdale, Florida, in 1995, where they opened a family business in healthcare in 1996.

Carla retired from her profession in 2017. Shortly thereafter, she decided to swim the legendary 12.5-mile race around Key West. She joined Swim Fort Lauderdale Masters swim team and met coach Marty Hendrick, who carefully trained her for the race. It was while she was training for Key West in a remote ocean location, that Carla learned of the Parkland school shootings. Heartbroken for all the victims, and for the loss of one of her own, a swimmer, Carla returned home to a grieving community. Later, she met Mitch and Annika Dworet, and learned about their exceptional family. Nick's story needed to be told, and Carla was compelled and honored to tell it.

Returning to swimming in 2018 was a glorious renaissance for Carla. She now actively competes in many U.S. Masters Swimming venues, including the pool. In the summer of 2018, Carla was the breaststroker on a women's medley relay which broke a Pan American record, a full-circle achievement back to 1976.

By the end of 2018, Carla had established several team records and was awarded one of the Great Strides Awards by Swim Fort Lauderdale Masters. In 2019 and 2020, Carla attained individual national top-10 awards in U.S. Masters competition.

Carla resides in Hollywood, Fla., with her husband, George Cann.

CPSIA information can be obtained
at www.ICGtesting.com
Printed in the USA
BVHW092126060522
636389BV00013B/194